HER *Blooming* SEASON

A Self-Care Journey to Heal, Reflect, and Blossom Into the **Best Version of You**

ZARA JONES

Book design by Callie Revell, callierevell.com

Published by LLD Legacy Publishing, LLC

Printed in the United States of America

To the one holding this book, this is your season to root yourself deeply. Even if growth feels slow, trust that you are building a foundation so strong that nothing will shake you. Flowers spend their first seasons establishing roots unseen beneath the soil. Your self-care journey may look the same: quiet, hidden, even uncertain. But when it is your time to bloom, you will rise, radiant and unshakable, into the beautiful flower you were always meant to be.

Contents

Dear Reader...

For those who don't know where to start or feel self-care is too far out of reach, I wrote this book for you. Years ago, after an accident left me lost and questioning my identity, I felt the same isolation, the same silence. But it was through small seeds of self-care that I found my way back.

Each pillar in this book carries a piece of that journey, and now it belongs to you, too. May these pages be your safe space to write your story alongside mine. To uproot what no longer serves you, to replant in richer soil, and to blossom in every season of your life.

This is for you as you learn to replant yourself, to uproot from the weeds, and to find new soil where you can truly grow. Your roots may be forming quietly now, unseen by the world, but they are the strength that will one day lift you into bloom. May these pages remind you: *growth is not always fast, but it is always worth the wait.*

With love and blooms,

Self-Love

SELF-LOVE

Introduction

Self-love is one of the most important and powerful relationships you'll ever have. It's not about being perfect or always feeling good about yourself. Instead, it's about accepting who you are, appreciating your uniqueness, and treating yourself with kindness, even when you make mistakes.

Self-love is more than just feeling happy when you look in the mirror. It's about learning to trust yourself, believe in your worth, and care for yourself in a way that makes you stronger and happier. It's an ongoing process, a journey that allows you to grow into the person you're meant to be.

Why Self-Love Matters

Self-love affects every part of your life. Without it, it's easy to feel like you're not good enough or to rely on others for approval and validation. You might end up saying yes to things you don't want, staying in unhealthy relationships, or doubting yourself constantly.

When you practice self-love, you stop looking for your worth in others. You start setting healthy boundaries, walking away from things that hurt you, and making decisions that align with what you truly need and want. Self-love gives you the courage to show up for yourself and live life on your terms.

It's also important to remember that self-love isn't selfish. In fact, it's the opposite. When you take care of yourself and learn to love who you are, you can be a better person, not just for yourself but for others too. You're able to give more to the people around you because you're not running on empty.

The Power of Self-Love

Learning to love yourself has the power to change your life. It doesn't mean you'll never feel insecure or face hard days. But when you love yourself, you can face those challenges with more strength and patience. You'll be able to silence your inner critic and replace it with a voice that's supportive and kind.

Self-love also helps you see your imperfections in a new light. Instead of trying to hide or "fix" them, you start to realize that they're part of what makes you special. You begin to see that your value isn't tied to how you look, what

you've achieved, or what others think of you—it comes from simply being you.

Self-Love vs. Selfishness

A lot of people confuse self-love with being selfish, but they're not the same. Selfishness is about putting yourself first while ignoring or harming others. Self-love is about taking care of yourself so you can show up as your best self for others.

When you love yourself, you're not asking the world to revolve around you. You're just recognizing your worth and giving yourself the care and respect you deserve. Self-love sets the standard for how others treat you. When you love yourself, you teach others that you deserve kindness, respect, and love.

My Journey to Self-Love

For much of my early teens, I struggled to love myself. Middle school and high school were particularly challenging, as I constantly pushed myself to achieve more, hoping it would make me feel seen, valued, and celebrated. Whether it was excelling in school, participating in extracurricular activities, or chasing recognition from teachers, peers, and even family, I thought my worth was tied to how much I could accomplish. I believed that if I could just achieve enough, people would notice me, praise me, and make me feel like I mattered.

But no matter how much I achieved, the fulfillment I craved never came. The applause would fade quickly, and I'd be left feeling empty, questioning if I had done enough

or if my accomplishments were even worth celebrating. I constantly raised the bar for myself, thinking that the next achievement would finally bring the validation I desired. Instead, I became trapped in a cycle of overworking, doubting myself, pushing myself way beyond my limits to burnout, and still feeling invisible.

On top of this, I struggled with my low hearing, which made me feel different in a way I thought was negative. I worried that my hearing made it harder for people to connect with me or see me as "normal." I thought it was another reason why I had to try harder, achieve more, and prove my worth to the people around me. I felt like if I wasn't perfect, I wouldn't be enough.

This mindset took a toll on me emotionally and mentally. I was constantly overthinking and placing so much pressure on myself to succeed, yet I still felt unseen. I thought my value was tied to what I could do rather than who I was. I was chasing external validation to fill an internal void, but no achievement ever truly filled it.

It wasn't until later that I started to realize the real problem wasn't that I wasn't achieving enough—it was that I wasn't giving myself the love and validation I deserved. I had been so focused on proving my worth to others that I completely overlooked the need to find that worth within myself. It hit me that no matter how much I accomplished, or how many titles and recognitions I had, it would never feel like enough if I didn't believe I was enough first.

I also began to reflect on my low hearing, which I had always seen as a weakness. Over time, I realized it wasn't a flaw at all—it was a unique part of who I am. It taught me to listen deeply, not just to people's words but to their emotions and energy. It helped me connect with others in ways I never noticed before. I even began to see it as a kind

of protection, allowing me to block out negativity and focus on what truly served me. What I once saw as a reason to hide became something I could appreciate about myself.

The journey to self-love wasn't quick or easy. It took time for me to shift my mindset and break free from the idea that my worth was tied to my achievements. I had to learn to separate what I do from who I am. I started focusing on smaller, meaningful steps—practicing self-compassion, celebrating myself without waiting for others to do it, and embracing the things about me that made me different.

I've come to understand that self-love is about more than just accepting your flaws. It's about recognizing your worth, not because of what you've accomplished, but simply because you exist. Achievements can be wonderful, but they aren't the foundation of your value. That value is already within you—it always has been.

Today, I no longer chase validation from others to feel fulfilled. I celebrate my wins because I'm proud of my efforts, not because I need recognition. I embrace my differences as part of what makes me unique, not as something that sets me apart in a negative way. Most importantly, I've learned that loving myself is the key to feeling whole. The external applause will fade, but the love I give to myself will always be enough.

A Message for You

Self-love isn't about being perfect or loving every single part of yourself all the time. It's about accepting who you are and choosing to care for yourself, even on the days you feel like you don't deserve it. You are worthy of love—not

because of what you do or how you look, but simply because you exist. Take this journey one day at a time, and remember: the relationship you build with yourself is the foundation for the life you create.

Day 1

"I am worthy of love, starting with the love I give myself."

I am learning to embrace the truth that the foundation of all love begins within me. For so long, I searched for validation and affection from others, believing that their approval was the key to feeling whole. But each day, I remind myself that the love I seek must first come from the way I care for and honor myself.

Loving myself means acknowledging my worth, even on the days when I feel imperfect. It means showing up for myself in ways that soothe my heart—whether through

kind words in the mirror, taking time to rest, or treating myself to moments that bring me joy.

I've come to understand that the love I give myself sets the standard for the love I invite into my life. When I nurture my heart, body, and soul, I radiate an energy that draws in relationships rooted in mutual respect and care. Today, I am choosing to practice self-compassion and self-acceptance. I am worthy of love—not because of what I achieve, how I look, or what I give to others—but simply because I am me.

By starting with self-love, I am building the foundation for a life filled with authentic, deep connections and a deeper sense of fulfillment.

Morning Prompt

What does self-love look like for you today?
Write one thing you'll do to honor yourself.

_____

_____

_____

_____

_____

_____

_____

_____

_____

_____

_____

_____

_____

_____

_____

_____

_____

Evening Prompt

How did you show love to yourself today?
What did you learn about your worth?

_____

_____

_____

_____

_____

_____

_____

_____

_____

_____

_____

_____

_____

_____

_____

_____

_____

_____

_____

Day 2

**"I choose to see myself through a lens
of kindness and compassion."**

Every day, I am presented with countless moments to reflect on who I am and how I show up in the world. In the past, I've often been my own harshest critic, quick to point out flaws, mistakes, or shortcomings. But today, I am choosing differently. I am learning to see myself with the same kindness I extend to a dear friend.

Through this lens of compassion, I remind myself that I am human—imperfect but perfectly imperfect. My mistakes are not failures; they are lessons that help me grow.

My struggles are not weaknesses; they are signs of my resilience. Each part of me, even the parts I once deemed unworthy, deserves understanding and care.

When I practice kindness toward myself, I feel a shift within me. My inner dialogue softens, and I feel more at ease with who I am. I let go of the weight of self-judgment and make space for encouragement and hope. Today, I will celebrate my efforts, no matter how small. I will honor my journey and recognize that every step forward, no matter how imperfect, is a step worth applauding.

Seeing myself through this lens of kindness and compassion doesn't mean ignoring areas where I can grow—it means embracing my journey with patience and love. It means holding space for the person I am now while nurturing the person I am becoming.

Morning Prompt

*What is one kind thought or compliment you can give
yourself to start the day?*

_____

_____

_____

_____

_____

_____

_____

_____

_____

_____

_____

_____

_____

_____

_____

_____

_____

_____

_____

_____

Evening Prompt

Did you speak kindly to yourself today?
Reflect on any critical moments and how you could reframe them.

_____

_____

_____

_____

_____

_____

_____

_____

_____

_____

_____

_____

_____

_____

_____

_____

_____

_____

_____

Day 3

**"My imperfections make me unique,
and I embrace them fully."**

For so long, I believed that my imperfections were flaws to be hidden or fixed. But as I continue to grow, I realize they are not weaknesses—they are the unique brushstrokes that paint the picture of who I am. My quirks, my differences, and my vulnerabilities tell a story that no one else can replicate. They remind me of my journey, my resilience, and the beauty in my individuality.

Embracing my imperfections doesn't mean I stop striving to grow or improve—it means I stop chasing an

unattainable idea of perfection. I allow myself to exist as I am, without shame or apology. These imperfections have taught me valuable lessons, deepened my empathy, and made me more relatable to others. They are what connect me to the world in an authentic way.

Today, I choose to stand tall in my truth, celebrating the parts of me that I once tried to hide. I no longer see imperfection as something to fear but as something to honor. It is in my imperfections that I find my greatest strength and my truest self.

By embracing all of who I am, I set myself free. Free to live, love, and grow without the weight of unrealistic expectations. Free to be unapologetically me—perfectly imperfect, and wonderfully unique.

Morning Prompt

What imperfection have you recently struggled to accept?
How could it add value to your journey?

_____

_____

_____

_____

_____

_____

_____

_____

_____

_____

_____

_____

_____

_____

_____

_____

_____

_____

_____

_____

_____

_____

Evening Prompt

Reflect on a moment today where you embraced or struggled with an imperfection. What did you learn?

_____

_____

_____

_____

_____

_____

_____

_____

_____

_____

_____

_____

_____

_____

_____

_____

_____

_____

_____

_____

_____

Day 4

"I am whole, just as I am."

There was a time when I believed that something was missing, that I needed to achieve more, change myself, or be someone different to feel complete. But the truth is, I have always been whole. Every part of me—my strengths and my struggles, my light and my shadows—comes together to create the beautiful, multifaceted person I am today.

Being whole doesn't mean I don't have room to grow. It means I am enough in this moment, even as I evolve. It means I honor my journey and trust that I am exactly

where I need to be right now. I don't need external valida-tion or achievements to define my worth; it comes from within.

Today, I choose to release the pressure to constantly fix or improve myself and instead embrace the peace that comes with knowing I am already complete. I will nurture my mind, body, and spirit, not because I am lacking, but because I deserve care and love in abundance.

By affirming my wholeness, I give myself permission to live fully and authentically. I no longer seek to fill a void, because there is none. I am whole, just as I am, and that is a powerful, unshakable truth.

Morning Prompt

*What would it feel like to move through the day
knowing you are already whole?*

_____

_____

_____

_____

_____

_____

_____

_____

_____

_____

_____

_____

_____

_____

_____

_____

_____

_____

Evening Prompt

What actions or thoughts today reflected your sense of wholeness?
Where could you improve?

_____

_____

_____

_____

_____

_____

_____

_____

_____

_____

_____

_____

_____

_____

_____

_____

_____

_____

_____

_____

_____

_____

Day 5

"I honor my boundaries because they protect my peace."

For too long, I hesitated to set boundaries, fearing they might make me seem selfish or unkind. But I've come to understand that boundaries are not walls—they are acts of self-respect and care. They are my way of telling the world, and myself, that my peace and well-being matter.

When I honor my boundaries, I create space for what truly nourishes me. I protect my energy from being drained by overcommitment or relationships that no longer serve me. I remind myself that it's okay to say no

when something doesn't align with my values or needs. By doing so, I am choosing to prioritize my mental, emotional, and spiritual health.

Setting and maintaining boundaries isn't always easy, but it's necessary. I've learned that when I honor my limits, I show others how to respect them as well. And when I hold firm to these boundaries, I find a sense of freedom and balance that allows me to thrive.

Today, I will continue to honor my boundaries without guilt or hesitation. They are not a sign of weakness but a reflection of my strength and self-worth. By protecting my peace, I can show up as my best self—for me and for those I care about.

Morning Prompt

*What boundary needs to be reinforced today
to protect your energy?*

_____

_____

_____

_____

_____

_____

_____

_____

_____

_____

_____

_____

_____

_____

_____

_____

_____

_____

_____

Evening Prompt

How did honoring your boundaries impact your day?
Did you encounter any challenges?

_____

_____

_____

_____

_____

_____

_____

_____

_____

_____

_____

_____

_____

_____

_____

_____

_____

_____

_____

_____

Resilience

RESILIENCE

Introduction

Resilience is the ability to bounce back from life's challenges and setbacks. It's the inner strength that allows you to keep going when everything around you feels uncertain or overwhelming.

Resilience doesn't mean you won't feel pain, frustration, or doubt—it means you find a way to rise again, even after you've fallen.

At its core, resilience is about adapting, learning, and growing through life's difficulties. It's about facing challenges head-on, even when they feel impossible, and finding the courage to move forward. Resilience helps us recognize that setbacks are not the end—they are part of the

process that makes us stronger, wiser, and more connected to our purpose.

Why Is Resilience Important?

Life is unpredictable, and everyone faces challenges. Whether it's a personal loss, a career setback, or a moment of self-doubt, these experiences can test us in ways we never imagined. Without resilience, it's easy to feel stuck, overwhelmed, or defeated. But resilience gives us the tools to keep going, even when the path is uncertain.

Resilience is more than just surviving tough times—it's about thriving through them. It helps us adapt to change, manage stress, and find meaning in our struggles.

With resilience, we're able to reflect on our experiences, learn from them, and come out stronger on the other side. It reminds us that we are capable of enduring more than we think and that even the most difficult moments can lead to growth.

The Power of Resilience

Resilience is not something you're born with—it's a skill that can be built over time. It's developed through the choices you make every day: choosing to get back up after a failure, to lean on your support system, and to give yourself the space to heal.

Resilience teaches you that taking a step back isn't giving up—it's part of the process of moving forward.

Resilience also helps you see challenges as opportunities for self-discovery. It encourages you to reflect on your strengths, recognize areas for growth, and build a deeper understanding of who you are. With resilience, you learn to trust yourself and your ability to handle whatever comes your way.

My Journey to Resilience

One of the biggest challenges I've faced was during my first year of high school. I was a basketball player, and sports weren't just a hobby for me—they were part of my identity. Basketball was a big part of my life and my household, and I had spent years playing and months preparing for tryouts. It wasn't just about making the team; it was about proving myself, building connections with my peers, and continuing something that had always been a part of me.

But just before tryouts, everything changed. I was in an accident that left me with kidney trauma, a lower back injury, and a concussion. I was forced into isolation to heal physically, but the emotional and mental toll was even harder to bear. I felt completely lost. I wasn't just missing the tryouts I had worked so hard for—I felt like I was losing my identity as a student-athlete. I was watching from the sidelines as my peers connected, built friendships, and created memories on and off the court. I felt excluded like I had missed my chance to belong.

On top of that, I felt like I was letting everyone down—my family, my teams, and myself. Sports and academics were incredibly important in my household, and being unable to play or even attend school made me feel like I wasn't living up to expectations. The pressure I placed on myself became overwhelming, and it was hard to stay motivated when my year had started with injury af-

ter injury.

At the time, I didn't think of myself as resilient. In fact, I didn't even know what resilience was. There were so many moments when I felt like giving up—on school, on basketball, and on myself. But looking back, I realize that even in my lowest moments, I never truly quit. I was resting. I was healing, physically and emotionally. I was taking the time I needed to figure out who I was beyond basketball.

I started to see that stepping back wasn't a failure—it was necessary. I wasn't giving up; I was making space to reevaluate what mattered to me. That accident, as devastating as it felt at the time, was a turning point. It forced me to ask deeper questions about my purpose and what I wanted for my life. It wasn't about abandoning basketball—it was about clearing the way for my true calling.

Resilience didn't come all at once. It was something I had to learn and practice. I began to focus on my mental and emotional health, to reflect on my strengths, and to give myself grace when things felt hard. I realized that resilience doesn't mean you don't feel pain or frustration—it means you keep moving forward despite it. It means learning from your challenges and allowing them to shape you in a positive way.

Resilience has completely shifted the way I approach challenges and setbacks. It has taught me that tough moments aren't the end—they're opportunities to grow and discover new strengths. Looking back on some of the hardest times in my life, like the accident that changed my high school experience, I can now see how those moments shaped me into the person I am today. Resilience gave me the courage to rebuild, adapt, and redefine my path when things didn't go the way I planned. It turned my struggles into stepping stones, allowing me to move forward with greater clarity and purpose.

One of the biggest lessons resilience has taught me is the value of rest and reflection. For a long time, I believed that pushing through every obstacle without pause was the only way to show strength. But I've learned that resilience doesn't mean ignoring your emotions or pretending everything is okay. It's about recognizing when you need to step back, recharge, and give yourself the space to heal. Taking that time to pause doesn't mean you're giving up—it means you're preparing yourself to come back stronger.

Resilience has also helped me to embrace change, even when it feels overwhelming. I've faced moments of heartbreak, self-doubt, and uncertainty, and each time, resilience has been the anchor that kept me grounded. Instead of fearing change, I've started to see it as an opportunity to grow and evolve. Challenges no longer feel like roadblocks; they've become reminders of my ability to adapt and keep moving forward. Through resilience, I've learned to trust myself and my ability to overcome whatever comes my way.

Another important shift I've noticed is how resilience has helped me find deeper meaning in my experiences. Instead of seeing my struggles as things to avoid or forget, I've started to see them as valuable parts of my story. Each challenge has taught me something about myself—my strengths, my values, and the areas where I still want to grow. Resilience has given me the tools to turn those lessons into action, helping me to build a life that reflects who I truly am.

For anyone looking to build resilience, I encourage you to start small, just as I did. Journaling was one of the first tools that helped me find my spark again. Writing down my thoughts and feelings gave me a safe space to process my emotions and reflect on what I was going through. Pairing journaling with affirmations allowed me to focus on my strengths and remind myself of my worth, even on the hardest days. These practices helped me reconnect with myself and build the inner strength I needed to move forward. Resilience is a skill you can develop, and it begins with small, intentional steps. By using tools like journaling and affirmations, you can start to build your resilience and discover your own spark within.

Day 6

"I have the strength to overcome any challenge that comes my way."

Life has a way of testing me with obstacles that feel overwhelming at times. Yet, each challenge I've faced has shown me just how resilient I am. I remind myself of the times I thought I couldn't make it through, but somehow, I did. Those moments have shaped me, strengthened me, and proved to me that I am capable of more than I often give myself credit for.

Challenges are not here to define me by my struggles but to refine me through my perseverance. They teach me

to adapt, to grow, and to find solutions even when the path seems unclear. I don't need to have all the answers right away—I trust in my ability to take one step at a time.

Today, I choose to see challenges not as barriers but as opportunities to discover my inner power. I have the courage to face difficulties head-on, the patience to navigate through uncertainty, and the wisdom to learn from every experience.

No matter what comes my way, I know I have the strength to overcome it. I carry within me a deep well of resilience, fueled by my belief in myself. With every challenge I face, I grow stronger, braver, and more capable of creating a life I'm proud of.

Morning Prompt

What potential challenges might arise today, and how can you prepare to face them with strength?

_____

_____

_____

_____

_____

_____

_____

_____

_____

_____

_____

_____

_____

_____

_____

_____

_____

_____

Evening Prompt

What challenges did you face today, and how did you show resilience in handling them?

_____

_____

_____

_____

_____

_____

_____

_____

_____

_____

_____

_____

_____

_____

_____

_____

_____

_____

_____

Day 7

"Each setback is an opportunity to grow stronger."

Setbacks can be tough to face—they often feel like roadblocks, derailing my plans and challenging my patience. But I've learned that every setback carries a lesson, a chance to grow in ways I might not have expected. They remind me that growth isn't always a straight line; it's a journey of resilience, adaptability, and self-discovery.

When I encounter setbacks, I take a moment to reflect on what they're teaching me. Sometimes, they push me to think creatively, to find a new path, or to dig deeper into my inner strength. Other times, they remind me to slow down, reevaluate, or approach a situation with a fresh perspective.

I remind myself that setbacks do not define my worth or my ability to succeed. Instead, they are stepping stones, helping me build the strength, courage, and wisdom I need to move forward. With each challenge I face, I become more resilient and more prepared for the journey ahead.

Today, I will embrace setbacks with grace and see them for what they truly are—opportunities to grow stronger. I trust that every obstacle is shaping me into the best version of myself. With patience, perseverance, and faith in my journey, I can overcome anything life places in my path.

Morning Prompt

Reflect on a past setback.
How can it serve as motivation for your day ahead?

_____

_____

_____

_____

_____

_____

_____

_____

_____

_____

_____

_____

_____

_____

_____

_____

_____

_____

_____

_____

Evening Prompt

Did you encounter any setbacks today?
What did you learn from them?

_____

_____

_____

_____

_____

_____

_____

_____

_____

_____

_____

_____

_____

_____

_____

_____

_____

_____

_____

Day 8

"My courage grows with every step I take outside my comfort zone."

Stepping outside of my comfort zone can feel intimidating, but I know it is where true growth begins. Each time I take a step into the unfamiliar, I remind myself that courage isn't the absence of fear—it's moving forward despite it. With every bold action, no matter how small, I prove to myself that I am capable of more than I once believed.

The moments when I challenge myself—whether it's speaking up, trying something new, or pursuing a dream—

are the moments when I feel most alive. They remind me that discomfort is not a sign to stop but a signal that I am growing. Each step I take expands my world, strengthens my confidence, and helps me discover parts of myself I never knew existed.

Today, I choose to embrace the unknown with an open heart and a curious spirit. I trust that even if things don't go perfectly, every experience teaches me something valuable. My courage grows not because the path is easy but because I am willing to walk it.

With every step outside my comfort zone, I become braver, stronger, and more aligned with the person I want to be. I carry this courage with me, knowing it will guide me to a life filled with growth, opportunity, and fulfillment.

Morning Prompt

What is one courageous step you can take today,
even if it feels uncomfortable?

_____

_____

_____

_____

_____

_____

_____

_____

_____

_____

_____

_____

_____

_____

_____

_____

_____

_____

_____

_____

_____

_____

Evening Prompt

What step outside your comfort zone did you take today?
How did it feel?

_____

_____

_____

_____

_____

_____

_____

_____

_____

_____

_____

_____

_____

_____

_____

_____

_____

_____

_____

_____

_____

Day 9

"I am proud of the progress I have made, no matter how small."

It's easy to get caught up in the big picture, comparing my journey to others or focusing on how far I still want to go. But today, I choose to honor every small step I've taken, because each one is a testament to my dedication and resilience. Progress isn't always loud or grand—it's often quiet and steady, and that is just as powerful.

Every step I've taken, no matter how small, has brought me closer to becoming the person I aspire to be. The moments when I chose to keep going, even when it felt hard, are proof of my strength. The tiny shifts I've made—choosing kindness over criticism, showing up for myself even when it wasn't easy—deserve to be celebrated.

Today, I will pause and acknowledge how far I've come. I'll recognize that progress isn't just about reaching the destination; it's about embracing the journey and the growth that comes with it. I am proud of myself for the effort I've put in, the lessons I've learned, and the courage I've shown to keep moving forward.

No matter how small the steps may seem, they are mine, and they are meaningful. Each one is a victory, a reminder that I am capable, and a sign that I am on the right path. I am proud of the progress I have made and excited for all the progress still to come.

Morning Prompt

What small accomplishment are you celebrating today?
How does it remind you of your progress?

_____

_____

_____

_____

_____

_____

_____

_____

_____

_____

_____

_____

_____

_____

_____

_____

_____

_____

_____

Evening Prompt

Reflect on your progress today.
What's one thing you're proud of, and why?

_____

_____

_____

_____

_____

_____

_____

_____

_____

_____

_____

_____

_____

_____

_____

_____

_____

_____

_____

_____

Day 10

"I have the power to turn my struggles into strength."

Life isn't always easy, and struggles are a part of the journey. At times, they may feel heavy, overwhelming, or unfair. But I've realized that within every challenge lies an opportunity—a chance to discover just how strong and capable I truly am. My struggles do not define me; how I rise above them does.

When I face adversity, I remind myself that it's okay to feel the weight of it, but I won't let it keep me down. Each difficulty I overcome teaches me resilience, patience, and perseverance. It shapes me, not into someone hardened by pain, but someone strengthened by growth. I choose to see my struggles as stepping stones, not roadblocks.

Today, I acknowledge the strength I've already gained from past challenges. They have equipped me with tools, wisdom, and the confidence to face whatever comes next. I honor the lessons I've learned and the person I'm becoming because of them.

I have the power to transform my struggles into strength by shifting my perspective, seeking solutions, and trusting in my ability to persevere. With each hardship I overcome, I grow more resilient and grounded in who I am. I am not just surviving—I am thriving, turning my pain into power and my struggles into strength.

Morning Prompt

What struggle are you currently facing, and how can you reframe it as an opportunity?

_____

_____

_____

_____

_____

_____

_____

_____

_____

_____

_____

_____

_____

_____

_____

_____

_____

_____

_____

_____

_____

Evening Prompt

*How did today's struggles make you stronger or
teach you something valuable?*

_____

_____

_____

_____

_____

_____

_____

_____

_____

_____

_____

_____

_____

_____

_____

_____

_____

_____

_____

_____

_____

Growth

GROWTH

Introduction

Growth is one of the most powerful transformations we experience in life. It is the process of learning, evolving, and becoming a better version of ourselves. Growth is not about perfection—it's about progress. It's about expanding our understanding, gaining new experiences, and learning from both our successes and our mistakes. Without growth, we remain stagnant, repeating the same patterns, stuck in the same mindset, and limiting ourselves from reaching our full potential.

Growth often comes from the lessons we learn through failure and hardship. Yet, for a long time, I was terrified of making mistakes. I feared failure, believing that it meant I

wasn't good enough or that I had somehow fallen behind. But I've learned that mistakes are not something to fear— they are a necessary part of the journey. Growth happens when we take risks, learn from our missteps, and continue moving forward despite the setbacks. It's not about avoiding failure, but about using it as a stepping stone to get to where we want to be.

Why Growth Is Important?

Growth is essential because without it, we remain stuck in old patterns, unable to reach the life we truly desire. It allows us to break free from limiting beliefs, challenge ourselves, and embrace the unknown. Growth pushes us outside of our comfort zones, forcing us to confront our fears, insecurities, and doubts. It shapes us into stronger, wiser individuals who are capable of handling life's uncertainties.

But growth is not always easy. It can be uncomfortable, even painful at times. It requires us to let go of things that no longer serve us—old habits, outdated mindsets, and sometimes even people. As we evolve, our perspectives shift, and the way we see life begins to change. This can mean outgrowing relationships, distancing ourselves from environments that no longer align with who we are becoming, and stepping into unfamiliar territory. It can feel isolating, but growth is necessary for a fulfilling life.

The truth is, nothing in life stays the same forever. We are constantly changing, whether we embrace it or not. When we lean into growth, instead of resisting it, we allow ourselves to reach new levels of success, happiness, and inner peace.

The Power of Growth

Growth is both exciting and uncomfortable. There were many times when I feared change because I didn't know what was waiting on the other side. I had to leave behind old ways of thinking, let go of familiar but unhealthy habits, and sometimes even distance myself from people who no longer aligned with my journey. That was one of the hardest lessons I had to learn.

I used to believe that growth meant leaving people behind in a painful way. I struggled with the idea that the friendships and connections I had built weren't meant to last forever. But as I started to evolve, I realized that not everyone grows at the same pace. Some people are comfortable staying the same, and that's okay—but I wasn't. I wanted to move forward, to surround myself with people who valued growth, self-improvement, and a life filled with positivity and purpose.

At first, it felt lonely. Growth often does. You start to question if you're making the right choices, if you're being "too much," if you should just settle for what's familiar. But the more I leaned into my growth, the more I realized that I was making space for something better. I was creating room for deeper, more fulfilling connections—friendships that supported my growth instead of holding me back. I was stepping into a version of myself that felt more authentic, more aligned with who I was meant to be.

My Journey to Growth

One of the biggest lessons I learned about growth came during a business class in college. My professor told

us something that stuck with me: In business, you will fail. You will make mistakes. You will hear "no" over and over again. But if you give up, how will you ever get to the "yes"? That lesson applies to life just as much as it does to business. Growth isn't about getting everything right the first time—it's about trying, failing, learning, and trying again.

For years, I was afraid of failure. I felt like I had to get everything right the first time, or it meant I wasn't good enough. But the truth is, without failure, we don't grow. We don't learn. We don't become stronger. Growth is what helps us move forward and reach our full potential. It's what allows us to break through the barriers that hold us back.

One of the hardest parts of my personal growth was learning to let go of the relationships that no longer served me. I held onto certain friendships because I wanted to stay close to people, even when I knew deep down that we were no longer aligned. I wanted to keep them in my life, even as I was evolving into someone who valued different things—positivity, self-improvement, and healthy, fulfilling connections. But I realized that some people weren't meant to grow with me.

They say, "It's lonely at the top," but I believe that it's lonely at the beginning of growth. You are shedding your old skin, stepping away from the familiar, and stepping into the unknown. But that loneliness isn't permanent. As you grow, you begin to attract new people—people who align with your values, who support your journey, and who uplift you rather than hold you back. Growth isn't just about reaching success; it's about creating a life that feels fulfilling, whole, and meaningful.

How You Can Use Growth as a Tool for Transformation

Growth is a lifelong journey, and it's one that you have control over. The first step to embracing growth is self-reflection. You have to take the time to understand where you are, what's holding you back, and what changes you need to make to move forward. That's why journaling became such a powerful tool for me. Writing helped me process my emotions, track my progress, and gain clarity on the lessons I was learning. It allowed me to see my growth in real-time and gave me the space to embrace change rather than fear it.

Along with journaling, I started practicing affirmations—reminding myself daily that growth is not something to fear, but something to celebrate. Affirmations helped me shift my mindset, replacing self-doubt with self-belief. They reminded me that change is a sign of progress, not loss.

Growth isn't always easy, but it is always worth it. No matter where you are in your journey, remember that you are not meant to stay the same forever. You are meant to evolve, to step into your fullest potential, and to create a life that truly reflects who you are. Use journaling, affirmations, and self-reflection as tools to guide your growth. Let go of what no longer serves you, embrace the discomfort of change, and trust that the best version of yourself is waiting on the other side.

Day 11

"I am always evolving into the best version of myself."

Life is a continuous journey of growth, and each day I take steps—big or small—toward becoming the person I am meant to be. I am not still; I am constantly learning, improving, and transforming. Even when I face setbacks, they are part of my evolution, teaching me lessons that guide me forward.

Becoming the best version of myself doesn't mean striving for perfection; it means embracing the process of growth with patience and grace. It means honoring who I

am today while working toward who I want to be tomorrow. I recognize that this journey is unique to me, and I celebrate every moment of progress along the way.

Today, I will take pride in my evolution. I will give myself credit for the effort I put into becoming more mindful, compassionate, and aligned with my true self. I trust that every experience—good or bad—is shaping me in meaningful ways.

I am not the same person I was yesterday, and I won't be the same tomorrow. I am always growing, healing, and moving closer to the best version of myself. With each choice I make, I step into my power, becoming stronger, wiser, and more fulfilled. My journey is a beautiful testament to the person I am becoming.

Morning Prompt

What does the best version of yourself look like today?
How can you embody that version of yourself through your
actions, mindset and choices?

_____

_____

_____

_____

_____

_____

_____

_____

_____

_____

_____

_____

_____

_____

_____

_____

_____

_____

_____

_____

Evening Prompt

How did you take a step toward growth today,
and what does that say about your evolution?

_____

_____

_____

_____

_____

_____

_____

_____

_____

_____

_____

_____

_____

_____

_____

_____

_____

_____

_____

_____

_____

_____

Day 12

"I trust the process, even when I can't see the entire path."

Life is a continuous journey of growth, and each day I take steps—big or small—toward becoming the person I am meant to be. I am not still; I am constantly learning, improving, and transforming. Even when I face setbacks, they are part of my evolution, teaching me lessons that guide me forward.

Becoming the best version of myself doesn't mean striving for perfection; it means embracing the process of growth with patience and grace. It means honoring who I

am today while working toward who I want to be tomorrow. I recognize that this journey is unique to me, and I celebrate every moment of progress along the way.

Today, I will take pride in my evolution. I will give myself credit for the effort I put into becoming more mindful, compassionate, and aligned with my true self. I trust that every experience—good or bad—is shaping me in meaningful ways.

I am not the same person I was yesterday, and I won't be the same tomorrow. I am always growing, healing, and moving closer to the best version of myself. With each choice I make, I step into my power, becoming stronger, wiser, and more fulfilled. My journey is a beautiful testament to the person I am becoming.

Morning Prompt

What area of your life requires more trust in the process?
How can you lean into it?

_____

_____

_____

_____

_____

_____

_____

_____

_____

_____

_____

_____

_____

_____

_____

_____

_____

_____

_____

_____

Evening Prompt

Did you trust yourself and the process today?
Reflect on the outcome.

_____

_____

_____

_____

_____

_____

_____

_____

_____

_____

_____

_____

_____

_____

_____

_____

_____

_____

_____

_____

_____

_____

Day 13

"I embrace change as a necessary part of growth."

Change can be unsettling, often taking me out of my comfort zone and into the unknown. But I've come to understand that change is not something to fear—it's a doorway to transformation. It's how I grow, evolve, and step into the person I'm meant to become.

Every change I face brings with it new opportunities, lessons, and perspectives. Even when it feels difficult, I remind myself that growth requires movement, and movement often requires letting go of what no longer serves

me. Change challenges me to adapt, to stretch, and to discover strengths I didn't know I had.

Today, I will welcome change with an open heart and mind. Instead of resisting it, I will see change as a gift— a chance to start fresh, explore new possibilities, and create a better version of my life. I trust that every shift, whether big or small, is happening for my highest good.

I embrace the uncertainty of change because I know it's a sign that I'm growing. Just as a flower needs to push through the soil to bloom, I need to move through change to reach my fullest potential. With each change I face, I am becoming more resilient, adaptable, and aligned with my purpose.

Morning Prompt

What change are you resisting?
How could embracing it help you grow?

Evening Prompt

What did you learn today about change,
and how did it shape you?

_____

_____

_____

_____

_____

_____

_____

_____

_____

_____

_____

_____

_____

_____

_____

_____

_____

_____

_____

_____

_____

_____

Day 14

"My mistakes are valuable lessons."

Mistakes are not failures—they are stepping stones on my journey of growth and self-discovery. Each mistake I've made has taught me something important about myself, the world, and the path I'm on. They remind me that I am human, and growth often comes from moments of imperfection.

Rather than dwelling on what went wrong, I choose to focus on what I can learn. Mistakes show me where I can improve, what I need to let go of, and how I can approach

things differently in the future. They are opportunities to build resilience, gain wisdom, and strengthen my character.

Today, I will approach my mistakes with curiosity and self-compassion. I won't let them define me or hold me back. Instead, I will use them as tools to refine my goals and clarify my direction. I understand that making mistakes is a natural part of progress, and they do not diminish my worth or potential.

With each mistake, I grow stronger, wiser, and more confident in my ability to navigate life. I am grateful for the lessons they bring, knowing that they are helping me become the best version of myself. My mistakes are not setbacks—they are stepping stones to success.

Morning Prompt

What recent mistake has been difficult to accept?
What lesson might it hold?

Evening Prompt

*What mistakes or missteps occurred today,
and what did they teach you?*

Day 15

"I am not afraid to try again, no matter how many times I fall."

Falling doesn't mean I've failed—it means I've tried, and that alone is an act of courage. Each time I stumble, I gain valuable insights that guide me closer to where I want to be. My strength is not in never falling, but in my willingness to rise again and keep moving forward.

The journey to success is rarely a straight line. I know that setbacks and challenges are part of the process, not the end of the road. Every time I choose to try again, I am proving to myself that my dreams and goals are worth the effort. I am not defined by my falls but by my determination to keep going.

Today, I will approach each setback with resilience and a renewed sense of purpose. I will release the fear of failure and embrace the courage to keep trying. With every attempt, I grow stronger, wiser, and more prepared for the opportunities ahead.

I trust that my persistence will lead to progress, even if it doesn't happen immediately. I am not afraid to start over, to learn from my experiences, and to try again, because I believe in my ability to succeed. No matter how many times I fall, I will always rise.

Morning Prompt

What is one area of your life where you need to try again?
What's holding you back?

_____

_____

_____

_____

_____

_____

_____

_____

_____

_____

_____

_____

_____

_____

_____

_____

_____

_____

_____

_____

_____

_____

Evening Prompt

What did you attempt today, and how did you grow from the experience, even if it didn't go as planned?

_____

_____

_____

_____

_____

_____

_____

_____

_____

_____

_____

_____

_____

_____

_____

_____

_____

_____

_____

_____

_____

Confidence

CONFIDENCE

Introduction

Confidence is not about being the loudest person in the room or always feeling fearless—it's about believing in yourself, even when the world tries to make you doubt your worth. True confidence comes from within, from knowing who you are, embracing your unique qualities, and refusing to let others define you.

But confidence isn't something we're born with—it's something we build. It's a skill that takes time, self-reflection, and practice. Many people think confidence means never feeling insecure, but that's not true. Even the most self-assured people have moments of doubt. The difference is that confident people don't let those doubts control

them. They stand firm in who they are, no matter what others say or think.

For a long time, I didn't believe I could be confident. I thought confidence was something other people had—people who were naturally outgoing, beautiful, or effortlessly charismatic. But what I've learned is that confidence isn't about being perfect. It's about being comfortable in your own skin, knowing your worth, and not letting external opinions dictate how you see yourself.

Why Confidence Is Important

Confidence is the foundation for living a fulfilling life. Without it, we constantly seek approval from others, doubt our decisions, and hold ourselves back from opportunities that could help us grow. When we lack confidence, we let fear control us—fear of failure, fear of judgment, fear of not being enough. But when we build confidence, we take control of our lives. We stop seeking validation and start living for ourselves.

Confidence allows us to speak up, take chances, and walk into any room knowing that we belong. It helps us set boundaries, stand up for ourselves, and navigate life without feeling the need to shrink ourselves to make others comfortable. It's not about arrogance or thinking you're better than anyone else—it's about knowing your own value and refusing to let anyone make you feel small.

The truth is, confidence isn't about eliminating insecurities. It's about learning to exist with them and not letting them define you. It's about embracing your uniqueness, rather than feeling ashamed of it.

The Power of Confidence

For much of my life, confidence felt out of reach. There were so many things I was insecure about—my appearance, the way I walked, how I always felt like I was behind, never quite where I wanted to be. But one of my deepest insecurities was my low hearing. It was something I couldn't change, yet it became the thing I was most ashamed of.

I was bullied for it. People, including adults, would make jokes at my expense, exaggerating their words, raising their voices, or making sarcastic remarks as if my hearing was a flaw they had to tolerate. I saw the frustration on people's faces when I had to ask them to repeat themselves, and each time, it chipped away at my confidence. I started to isolate myself, avoiding conversations, staying quiet even when I had something to say—just so I wouldn't be an inconvenience.

But something changed when I started playing basketball. Somehow, the sport helped me find my voice. On the court, I had no choice but to communicate—I had to call plays, direct my teammates, and speak up if I wanted to be heard. It forced me to stop hiding. And through basketball, I learned that my voice mattered. I learned that I wasn't defined by my hearing, my insecurities, or by how others saw me. Slowly, I started carrying that same confidence off the court, into my everyday life.

Growing up, it was easy for me to stand up for my friends, to defend the people I cared about. But when it came to standing up for myself, it felt like an impossible battle. I had spent so much time trying to avoid being a burden, trying not to draw attention to my insecurities, that I forgot I had a right to be heard. Basketball was the first

step in changing that, but the real shift happened when I started changing how I spoke to myself.

My Journey to Confidence

One of the biggest lessons I've learned about confidence is that most insecurities don't come from us—they come from other people. For years, I believed there was something wrong with the way I walked, the way I talked, or even the way I dressed. But when I took a step back and asked myself why I felt that way, I realized those insecurities didn't come from me. They came from the opinions, jokes, and comments of others.

I realized that people will always have something to say. Some people project their own insecurities onto others, criticizing what makes you different because they haven't learned to embrace their own uniqueness. The quicker I learned to stop taking other people's words personally, the more I was able to step into my own confidence.

Confidence isn't about "fixing" yourself to meet other people's expectations. It's about accepting yourself as you are and recognizing that other people's opinions do not define your worth. Yes, we can always grow, evolve, and improve—but we should do it for ourselves, not because someone else has made us feel like we're not enough.

The moment I stopped worrying about how others saw me and started focusing on how I saw myself, everything changed. I started dressing in a way that made me feel good. I stopped overthinking how I walked, how I spoke, how I moved through the world. I started to understand that confidence isn't about being perfect—it's about being real.

How You Can Build Confidence in Your Own Life

Building confidence takes time, but it starts with self-awareness. Ask yourself where your insecurities come from. Are they things you believe, or are they things you've been told? Journaling helped me uncover this for myself. Writing down my thoughts and reflecting on where my self-doubt was coming from allowed me to take control of my own narrative.

Affirmations also became a key part of my confidence journey. I started replacing negative self-talk with words of encouragement. Instead of focusing on what I lacked, I focused on what I had. I reminded myself daily that I was enough, that my voice mattered, and that I didn't have to shrink myself to make others comfortable.

Confidence is something you build every single day. It's in the way you talk to yourself, the way you show up for yourself, and the way you refuse to let the world tell you who you are. The more you practice self-acceptance, the more confidence becomes second nature.

So if you're struggling with confidence, know this—you are not alone. But you are also not powerless. You have the ability to shift your mindset, to step into your worth, and to own who you are. And once you do, you'll realize that confidence was never about being perfect. It was about finally giving yourself permission to take up space, unapologetically.

Day 16

"I believe in myself and my abilities."

There is a quiet strength in believing in myself, even when the world feels uncertain. I remind myself that I have everything I need within me to achieve my goals and overcome any challenge. My abilities, my determination, and my unique perspective are all tools that empower me to move forward with confidence.

Believing in myself doesn't mean I'll never face doubts or setbacks—it means I trust that I can navigate them. It means I recognize my worth and acknowledge my capacity to grow, learn, and adapt. I honor the progress I've already

made and trust in my ability to continue moving toward my dreams.

Today, I choose to affirm my strengths and capabilities. I am capable of achieving great things when I put my heart and mind into them. I will face challenges with courage, knowing that I am equipped to handle whatever comes my way.

By believing in myself, I am opening the door to endless possibilities. My confidence becomes my foundation, and my abilities become the tools I use to build the life I desire. I am proud of who I am and excited about what I can achieve.

Morning Prompt

What ability are you most confident in today?
How can you use it to your advantage?

_____

_____

_____

_____

_____

_____

_____

_____

_____

_____

_____

_____

_____

_____

_____

_____

_____

_____

_____

_____

_____

Evening Prompt

How did you show confidence in yourself today?
What did it feel like?

_____

_____

_____

_____

_____

_____

_____

_____

_____

_____

_____

_____

_____

_____

_____

_____

_____

_____

_____

_____

Day 17

"My voice and presence matter."

I remind myself that I am here for a reason, and the world is better because of who I am. My thoughts, feelings, and ideas hold value, and my voice has the power to inspire, uplift, and create change. Whether I speak softly or boldly, my voice carries weight, and what I have to say matters.

There have been times when I've questioned my worth or felt invisible, but I know now that my presence leaves an imprint. Simply by being myself, I bring something unique and irreplaceable to every space I enter. My energy, my

compassion, and my perspective are gifts that others can benefit from.

Today, I will embrace the truth that I have a right to be heard and seen. I will speak with confidence, knowing that my words can create connection and understanding. I will show up fully and authentically, allowing my presence to shine without fear or hesitation.

By honoring my voice and presence, I am affirming my worth and contributing to the world in meaningful ways. I matter, and the spaces I occupy are richer because I am in them. My voice and presence are powerful, and I will never underestimate their importance.

Morning Prompt

How can you use your voice to make an impact today?

_____

_____

_____

_____

_____

_____

_____

_____

_____

_____

_____

_____

_____

_____

_____

_____

_____

_____

_____

_____

Evening Prompt

In what ways did you allow yourself to be seen and heard today?

_____

_____

_____

_____

_____

_____

_____

_____

_____

_____

_____

_____

_____

_____

_____

_____

_____

_____

_____

_____

Day 18

"I radiate confidence and self-assurance."

Confidence is not about being perfect—it's about trusting in myself and showing up authentically. When I walk into a room, I carry an inner light that shines from my belief in who I am and what I'm capable of. My confidence is not arrogance; it's a quiet, steady assurance that I am enough just as I am.

I've learned that self-assurance begins with the way I speak to myself. When I affirm my worth, embrace my strengths, and honor my journey, I feel a shift within me—

a powerful sense of self-belief that others can see and feel. This confidence isn't dependent on external validation; it comes from knowing my value and embracing my uniqueness.

Today, I will move through the world with my head held high and my heart open. I will take on challenges with courage, knowing that I am capable of handling them. I will celebrate my successes, no matter how small, and learn from every experience, which only strengthens my confidence further.

By radiating confidence and self-assurance, I am creating opportunities for growth and connection. My energy inspires others and invites positivity into my life. I am proud of who I am, and I trust that my confidence will guide me toward all that I deserve.

Morning Prompt

*What would it look like to walk through your day
with complete confidence?*

_____
_____
_____
_____
_____
_____
_____
_____
_____
_____
_____
_____
_____
_____
_____
_____
_____
_____
_____
_____
_____

Evening Prompt

Reflect on a moment today when you felt self-assured.
How can you carry that energy forward?

Day 19

"I am bold and fearless in the pursuit of my dreams."

Dreams require courage—the courage to take risks, face challenges, and step into the unknown. I remind myself that my dreams are worth the effort, and I have everything within me to pursue them with boldness and determination. Fear may try to hold me back, but I choose to move forward anyway, trusting in my ability to navigate the journey ahead.

Being fearless doesn't mean I'll never feel doubt or uncertainty—it means I refuse to let those feelings stop me.

Each step I take, no matter how small, is a declaration of my commitment to my dreams. I embrace the possibilities that come with daring to go after what I truly desire.

Today, I will take bold action toward my goals, knowing that every effort brings me closer to the life I envision. I will trust in my abilities and remain focused on my purpose, even when the path feels challenging. I am not afraid to try, to fail, or to learn, because I know each experience strengthens me.

By pursuing my dreams with courage, I am creating a life of passion, fulfillment, and authenticity. I am bold, fearless, and unstoppable, and I am proud of the journey I am on. My dreams are not just possibilities—they are inevitable because I have the power to make them real.

Morning Prompt

What bold action can you take today to move closer to your dreams?

_____

_____

_____

_____

_____

_____

_____

_____

_____

_____

_____

_____

_____

_____

_____

_____

_____

_____

_____

_____

_____

_____

Evening Prompt

How did you fearlessly pursue your dreams today?
What fueled your courage?

_____

_____

_____

_____

_____

_____

_____

_____

_____

_____

_____

_____

_____

_____

_____

_____

_____

_____

_____

_____

_____

_____

Day 20

"I am enough, exactly as I am."

In a world that often pushes me to strive for more, it's easy to forget that who I am right now is already worthy and whole. I don't need to earn my worthiness or prove myself to anyone—I am enough simply because I exist. My value isn't tied to what I achieve, how I look, or what others think of me.

Accepting that I am enough doesn't mean I won't continue to grow or evolve—it means I can embrace myself fully along the way. I honor my journey, with all its twists and turns, knowing that every part of me deserves love

and compassion. Even on my hardest days, when doubt creeps in, I remind myself that I am deserving of kindness, care, and respect.

Today, I will release the need to compare myself to others or chase perfection. Instead, I will celebrate the person I am right now, flaws and all. I will speak to myself with love and recognize the unique gifts I bring to the world.

By affirming that I am enough, I give myself the freedom to live authentically and unapologetically. I am whole, worthy, and deserving of all the good in life—just as I am.

Morning Prompt

*What does being "enough" mean to you today?
How can you remind yourself of this truth?*

_____

_____

_____

_____

_____

_____

_____

_____

_____

_____

_____

_____

_____

_____

_____

_____

_____

_____

_____

_____

Evening Prompt

How did you embrace the belief that you are enough today?
Where did you struggle?

Inner Peace

INNER PEACE

Introduction

Inner peace is more than just a moment of silence or relaxation—it's a state of being. It's the ability to remain calm and centered no matter what's happening around you. It doesn't mean life is free from challenges, stress, or conflict, but rather that you've built the resilience to handle them without letting them shake your core. Inner peace is about maintaining balance, not just reacting to situations, but responding in a way that serves you.

For me, inner peace goes hand in hand with resilience. It's not about avoiding problems or suppressing emotions—it's about learning to navigate difficulties with a steady mind. I've always tried to approach obstacles with a calm

and levelheaded mindset, looking at different perspectives to better understand situations. But I'll admit, sometimes that's easier said than done. There have been moments when stress, exhaustion, or overstimulation got the best of me, making me react in ways I normally wouldn't. Learning how to maintain my peace even in difficult moments has been one of the most valuable lessons in my journey.

Why Inner Peace Is Important

Inner peace is what allows us to move through life without feeling constantly overwhelmed. When we lack peace, even small inconveniences can feel like the end of the world. Our emotions become reactive, we start over-thinking, and our ability to handle challenges with clarity disappears. Without inner peace, we're more likely to seek external validation, compare ourselves to others, or push ourselves beyond our limits in an attempt to prove something to the world. But the truth is, inner peace isn't found in external achievements—it's something we create within ourselves.

The things that disrupt our inner peace aren't always major life events. Sometimes, they're the little things that build up over time—stress from work, feeling unappreciated, being overly critical of ourselves, or even just skipping meals and running on empty. I've noticed that when I'm already stressed, tired, and hungry, even the smallest inconvenience can feel ten times worse.

In those moments, my reactions don't reflect who I truly am—they're just a result of being overstimulated and not taking care of myself. That's why protecting your peace isn't just about handling big challenges—it's about recog-

nizing when your mind and body need rest and nourishment.

The Power of Inner Peace

Inner peace gives us the ability to stay grounded even when everything around us feels chaotic. When our minds are calm, we think more clearly, make better decisions, and approach challenges with a solution-oriented mindset instead of reacting impulsively. Inner peace isn't just about feeling good—it's about functioning better in every area of life.

One of the most eye-opening experiences for me was witnessing the struggle of a friend who was caught in a cycle of external pressure and self-doubt. They had just started a new job, and instead of allowing themselves time to learn and adjust, they were consumed with the need for instant validation. They wanted to prove themselves immediately, to be seen as successful, to meet unrealistic expectations that others had placed on them. No matter how much I reassured them that growth takes time and that they were doing better than they thought, they couldn't hear it. I understood that feeling all too well—because I've been there too.

When there's too much chaos—whether it's internal or external—our minds go into tunnel vision mode. We get stuck in cycles of overthinking, self-doubt, and frustration. We stop listening to logic and become consumed by what we think we should be doing, rather than honoring where we are. Seeing my friend go through that made me reflect on my own struggles with peace, the moments when I had let outside pressures dictate my emotions. It made me real-

ize that finding peace is not about controlling everything—
it's about learning to detach from the things that disrupt
our balance.

My Journey to Inner Peace

For a long time, I didn't realize how much I needed to
protect my peace. I used to believe that as long as I was
pushing through, I was doing okay. But over time, I noticed how exhaustion, stress, and overstimulation affected
my mood, my focus, and my ability to handle challenges. I
learned the hard way that if I didn't actively create peace in
my life, the world would never slow down for me.

One of the biggest shifts for me was implementing intentional quiet time into my daily routine. I started setting
aside an hour in the morning and another before bed—no
talking, no interactions, just time to be with myself.
Whether it was drinking tea, journaling, working out, meditating, or simply sitting in silence, these moments allowed
me to reset. I realized that the calmer my mind was, the
better I handled pressure. I wasn't as reactive. I didn't take
things as personally. And most importantly, I stopped letting small inconveniences ruin my entire day.

Another key lesson I learned was how much our environment influences our peace. Who we surround ourselves
with, the conversations we entertain, and the energy we allow into our space all play a role in our inner balance. I had
to start filtering what I consumed—whether that was negative self-talk, unnecessary drama, or situations that
drained me. The more I prioritized my peace, the more I
realized that I deserved it.

How You Can Cultivate Inner Peace

Inner peace is something you create, not something you wait for. It's about making intentional choices that help you feel calm, balanced, and centered. One of the best ways to start is by practicing self-awareness. Pay attention to what disrupts your peace—whether it's certain people, environments, habits, or even your own thoughts. Once you identify these triggers, you can start making small changes to protect your energy.

Journaling became one of the most powerful tools for me in maintaining inner peace. Writing helped me process my emotions, clear my mind, and reflect on the things that were weighing me down. It allowed me to separate what really mattered from what was just temporary stress. Pairing journaling with affirmations also helped me rewire my thinking. Instead of waking up and immediately worrying about what I needed to do or what others expected from me, I started my mornings by reminding myself that I am in control of my peace.

Inner peace isn't about escaping from reality—it's about creating a space within yourself that nothing external can shake. Life will always have challenges, but when you build a strong foundation of peace, you'll be able to face them with clarity and confidence. Start small. Give yourself time in the morning or at night to be with yourself. Set boundaries that protect your energy. And most importantly, remind yourself that peace is not a privilege—it's a choice. You deserve to move through life with ease, grace, and a mind that feels like home.

Day 21

"I let go of what I cannot control."

There is peace in surrendering what is beyond my reach. For too long, I've held onto worries, frustrations, and outcomes I couldn't change, believing that holding on would somehow make things better. But I've learned that true strength lies in letting go, in trusting that some things are simply not mine to carry.

Letting go doesn't mean I'm giving up—it means I'm freeing myself from the weight of unnecessary stress. It's a reminder that I can only control my own actions, words, and mindset. The rest is out of my hands, and that's okay. I trust that what is meant to be will unfold in its own time.

Today, I will release the need to control every detail and instead focus on what I can influence: my responses, my effort, and my attitude. I will shift my energy toward the things that bring me joy, peace, and fulfillment. Letting go opens the door for new opportunities and clarity to enter my life.

By letting go of what I cannot control, I create space for peace, resilience, and growth. I trust the process and know that I have the strength to navigate whatever comes my way. I am lighter, freer, and more grounded because I choose to let go.

Morning Prompt

What is one thing you need to release today to maintain your peace?

_____

_____

_____

_____

_____

_____

_____

_____

_____

_____

_____

_____

_____

_____

_____

_____

_____

_____

_____

_____

_____

_____

Evening Prompt

What did you hold onto today that you could have let go of?
How will you release it now?

Day 22

"My peace is my priority."

In a world full of noise and demands, I recognize the importance of protecting my inner calm. My peace is not a luxury—it is a necessity for my well-being. I understand that when I prioritize my peace, I am better able to show up for myself and others with clarity, patience, and love.

Choosing peace means setting boundaries that honor my needs, saying no when it's necessary, and removing myself from situations that drain my energy. It's a reminder that I don't have to engage in every conflict or respond to every external pressure. I have the power to choose where I place my energy and focus.

Today, I will create moments of stillness and mindfulness, nurturing the quiet spaces where I feel most grounded. I will let go of what doesn't serve me and embrace the things that bring me joy, balance, and harmony. Whether it's a deep breath, a walk in nature, or simply stepping away from stress, I will protect my peace unapologetically.

By prioritizing my peace, I am choosing myself. I am choosing to live a life that feels aligned and fulfilling. My peace is my power, and I will guard it with care and intention.

Morning Prompt

How can you protect your peace today, even in stressful situations?

_____

_____

_____

_____

_____

_____

_____

_____

_____

_____

_____

_____

_____

_____

_____

_____

_____

_____

_____

_____

Evening Prompt

Reflect on how well you prioritized peace today.
What will you do differently tomorrow?

_____

_____

_____

_____

_____

_____

_____

_____

_____

_____

_____

_____

_____

_____

_____

_____

_____

_____

_____

_____

_____

Day 23

"I create space for stillness and reflection."

In the busyness of life, it's easy to forget the importance of pausing. But I know that stillness is where clarity begins and reflection is where growth takes root. By creating space for quiet moments, I give myself the opportunity to reconnect with my thoughts, emotions, and intentions.

Stillness allows me to tune out the external noise and tune into my inner world. It's in these moments that I find balance, recharge my spirit, and gain a deeper understanding of myself. Reflection helps me process my experiences, celebrate my progress, and identify areas where I can grow.

Today, I will set aside time for stillness, even if it's just a few minutes. Whether through deep breathing, journaling, meditation, or simply sitting in silence, I will honor this time as sacred. I will use it to listen to my heart, appreciate the present, and align with my purpose.

By creating space for stillness and reflection, I nurture my mind, body, and soul. These moments of quiet are not a pause in my journey—they are a vital part of it. They allow me to move forward with intention, clarity, and a greater sense of peace.

Morning Prompt

What would creating space for stillness look like today?
How will it benefit you?

_____

_____

_____

_____

_____

_____

_____

_____

_____

_____

_____

_____

_____

_____

_____

_____

_____

_____

_____

_____

_____

Evening Prompt

When did you find moments of stillness today?
How did it impact your mindset?

Day 24

"I center myself with each breath, finding calm and stability within."

No matter what is happening around me, my breath is a constant source of grounding and peace. With each inhale, I draw in calm and clarity, and with each exhale, I release tension and worry. My breath connects me to the present moment, reminding me that stability comes from within.

When life feels overwhelming or uncertain, I can always return to my breath to find balance. Each breath anchors me, helping me stay rooted in my strength and resilience. I trust in my ability to find calm, even in the midst of chaos, simply by tuning into the rhythm of my breathing.

Today, I will take intentional moments to pause and breathe deeply. With every breath, I will center myself, letting go of distractions and reconnecting with my inner peace. My breath is my guide, leading me back to stability and clarity whenever I need it.

By centering myself through my breath, I create a strong foundation of calm and control. I am steady, grounded, and at ease, no matter what challenges arise. My breath is my power, and I use it to cultivate balance and harmony within.

Morning Prompt

What grounding practice can you incorporate into your day today?

_____

_____

_____

_____

_____

_____

_____

_____

_____

_____

_____

_____

_____

_____

_____

_____

_____

_____

_____

_____

_____

Evening Prompt

How did grounding yourself affect your emotions
and reactions today?

_____
_____
_____
_____
_____
_____
_____
_____
_____
_____
_____
_____
_____
_____
_____
_____
_____
_____
_____
_____
_____

Day 25

"I am at peace with where I am and excited about where I am going."

Life is a journey, and I honor the path I'm on. Right now, I choose to embrace this moment and find gratitude in where I am. I may not have everything figured out, but that's okay. Each step I've taken has brought me to this point, and I trust that I am exactly where I need to be.

Being at peace with where I am doesn't mean I'm settling—it means I'm releasing unnecessary stress and appreciating the present. I know that growth takes time, and I'm excited about the possibilities that lie ahead. My dreams and goals are within reach, and I am moving toward them with intention and confidence.

Today, I will celebrate my progress and trust the process. I will acknowledge the lessons I've learned and the strength I've gained along the way. I will let go of comparing my journey to others and focus on my unique path.

By finding peace in the present and excitement for the future, I align myself with a sense of purpose and joy. I am grateful for how far I've come, and I am ready for all the wonderful things that are yet to come. My journey is unfolding beautifully, and I am exactly where I am meant to be.

Morning Prompt

What about your current journey brings you peace?
What excites you about the future?

_____

_____

_____

_____

_____

_____

_____

_____

_____

_____

_____

_____

_____

_____

_____

_____

_____

_____

_____

_____

_____

_____

Evening Prompt

How did today bring you closer to inner peace and your future goals?

_____

_____

_____

_____

_____

_____

_____

_____

_____

_____

_____

_____

_____

_____

_____

_____

_____

_____

_____

_____

_____

Self-Worth

SELF-WORTH

Introduction

Self-worth is the foundation of how we see ourselves, how we treat ourselves, and what we allow into our lives. It's not based on what you've accomplished, what others think of you, or what you've been through—it's about recognizing your value simply because you exist. Self-worth is about knowing you are enough, just as you are—not because of a title you hold, a role you play, or a label someone else gave you, but because your presence, your story, and your heart matter.

I've spent years navigating self-worth—especially in moments when I doubted it the most. Any time I was presented with a new opportunity or a new environment, I

questioned myself: Am I good enough for this? What if I fail? What if I don't belong here? I would shrink myself in fear of not living up to people's expectations, or worse, letting them down. A lot of that fear came from not knowing how things would turn out, and assuming I wasn't the "right" person for the challenge. What I didn't realize then is that self-worth has nothing to do with fitting in and everything to do with showing up as you are.

Why Self-Worth Is So Important

Without self-worth, we let the world determine how we see ourselves. We believe we have to earn our place in relationships, at jobs, in social circles. We start attaching our value to titles—student, athlete, daughter, friend, entrepreneur—and when those titles shift or are taken away, we feel like we've lost ourselves. But your worth is not in the roles you play or the achievements you check off a list. You are not defined by your title. You are not defined by your productivity. And you are certainly not defined by your past.

This is where many people get stuck—believing that past mistakes, regrets, or moments of shame determine how worthy they are today. But the truth is, your past doesn't reduce your worth. If anything, the fact that you've been through difficult seasons and are still here, still trying, still growing—that speaks volumes about your strength. Self-worth is about owning your story, not erasing it. You are allowed to move forward, to heal, to grow into someone new. Your past is part of your path, but it doesn't get to write your future unless you let it.

My Journey to Rebuilding Self-Worth

There was a time in my life where I felt like I wasn't capable of stepping into new spaces. I questioned everything—my abilities, my value, my place in this world. I was afraid of change, not because I didn't want better for myself, but because I doubted that I was strong enough to handle it. That fear made me shrink. But the turning point came when I realized I didn't have to go through that alone.

I surrounded myself with people who saw the best in me even when I couldn't see it in myself. People who didn't judge or criticize, but instead poured into me—reminding me of my strength, my potential, and the version of me I was still becoming. I used to think I had to rebuild myself in isolation, but the truth is, we are deeply shaped by the energy we surround ourselves with. When I combined that support with daily reminders to myself—simple truths like "I am capable," "Every day is preparing me,"—I slowly started believing it.

One of the most powerful pieces of advice I received during this time was, "If you weren't capable of overcoming this, you would have never been placed in it." That changed how I viewed pressure, uncertainty, and fear. I started to understand that the challenges I faced weren't a sign that I was unworthy—they were part of the shaping process. They were revealing my strength, not my weakness.

How Self-Worth Changes Everything

Recognizing your worth affects every area of your life—from your friendships and relationships to your goals and your career. As a self-care advocate, my ability to show up for others depends on how I see myself. And while I still have moments of doubt, I now know that I don't have to be perfect to be powerful. I can hold space for others because I've learned to hold space for myself first. And I know now that what makes me relatable isn't having it all figured out—it's being willing to grow and be honest about the journey.

That same self-worth has helped me connect with others on deeper levels. I used to see my low hearing as something that separated me from people. But over time, I realized that being vulnerable about it often led to the most meaningful moments. I've had people light up when I shared my story and say, "Me too." That's the magic of self-worth—it allows you to embrace the parts of yourself you used to hide and use them to build bridges of connection. What you once saw as your weakness could be the very thing that makes someone else feel seen.

Self-worth, when embraced, becomes a ripple effect. When you know your worth, you give others permission to start valuing theirs too. It becomes less about performing and more about being. Less about impressing others and more about accepting yourself. And that creates space for relationships, environments, and opportunities that align with the real you—not the watered-down version created to please others.

How You Can Begin Reclaiming Your Self-Worth

If you're in a season of doubting your worth, I want to remind you: You are not your mistakes. You are not your titles. You are not your past. You are a full, complex, beautiful human being who is constantly evolving. Your worth is not measured by what others see—it is something you must begin to recognize and claim for yourself.

Start small. Surround yourself with people who uplift you. Create quiet space for reflection.

If you're in a season of doubting your worth, I want to remind you of something gentle yet powerful: You are not your mistakes. You are not your titles. You are not your past. You are not the version of yourself that made decisions from a place of fear, confusion, or pain. You are not the labels others have placed on you, nor the roles you've had to play to survive. You are a full, complex, beautiful human being who is constantly growing and evolving. You were never meant to stay the same. And your worth? It's not something you have to earn—it's already yours.

But I know firsthand that reclaiming your self-worth after years of doubt, criticism, or feeling unseen doesn't happen overnight. It's a gradual process, one that starts with giving yourself permission to heal. It starts by letting go of the idea that you need to be perfect to be valuable. That your past disqualifies you. Or that you have to shrink yourself to be accepted. The journey back to your worth begins with small, intentional steps—steps that center you, nourish you, and remind you of who you truly are underneath the pressure, the pain, and the performance.

Start small. Truly. Surround yourself with people who see you—not the filtered, performative version of you—

but the real you. The "I'm still figuring it out" version. The one who cries sometimes, who gets overwhelmed, who doesn't always know what to do next. These people won't fix your self-worth for you, but they'll reflect it back to you in moments you forget. Create space in your life for quiet reflection—journaling, sitting in silence, repeating affirmations that remind you of your power. Not because you have to, but because you deserve to. These habits aren't just routines—they're daily acts of self-remembrance.

Remind yourself that every experience, even the ones that broke your heart or shook your confidence, are not signs of failure. They are part of your shaping. Part of your becoming. You are allowed to outgrow who you once were. You're allowed to walk away from versions of yourself that you've outlived. That isn't fake. That isn't disloyal. That's what freedom looks like. Reclaiming your self-worth means trusting yourself again. Trusting that you can make decisions based on what you need, not just what others expect.

Self-worth isn't about proving anything. It's about unlearning the lies you were told and remembering the truth that's always been inside you: You are enough. You always have been. You always will be. So start living like it. Speak it over yourself, even when you don't feel it yet. Show up for yourself in ways that remind your spirit that you're worth the love, the rest, the kindness, the opportunities, and the joy you've been seeking. You don't have to chase it anymore. It starts with believing you already have it—and building from there.

Day 26

"I am deserving of happiness and success."

Happiness and success are not things I need to earn—they are my birthright. I remind myself that I am worthy of joy, fulfillment, and all the good things life has to offer simply because I exist. My past doesn't define me, and I don't have to prove my worth to anyone, including myself.

Being deserving means allowing myself to embrace opportunities, celebrate my wins, and find joy in the everyday moments. It means letting go of any guilt or doubt that tells me I'm not enough. I trust that my hard work, re-

silience, and positive energy will continue to attract success and happiness into my life.

Today, I will focus on what makes me feel truly happy and aligned with my purpose. I will recognize and celebrate my achievements, no matter how big or small. I will take steps toward my goals with confidence, knowing that I am fully deserving of reaching them.

By affirming my worthiness, I am opening myself to abundance and possibilities. Happiness and success are not distant dreams—they are present and attainable realities. I am ready to receive all the blessings life has in store for me because I know I am deserving of every single one.

Morning Prompt

What does happiness and success mean to you today?
How can you pursue it with confidence?

_____

_____

_____

_____

_____

_____

_____

_____

_____

_____

_____

_____

_____

_____

_____

_____

_____

_____

_____

_____

_____

Evening Prompt

How did you affirm your deservingness of joy and success today?

_____

_____

_____

_____

_____

_____

_____

_____

_____

_____

_____

_____

_____

_____

_____

_____

_____

_____

_____

_____

_____

Day 27

"I am not defined by others' opinions of me."

I am more than the labels, judgments, or perceptions others may place upon me. My worth is not determined by how others see me, but by how I see myself. I choose to define who I am based on my own values, experiences, and aspirations.

Others' opinions are shaped by their own perspectives and not a true reflection of my character or potential. I release the need to seek validation from others and instead focus on building a strong, unshakable sense of self. My

value doesn't waver based on praise or criticism—I remain whole and worthy regardless.

Today, I will remind myself that I have the power to choose what I internalize. I will listen to my own voice and trust in the person I am becoming. I will let go of the weight of others' judgments and focus on living authentically and true to myself.

By freeing myself from the opinions of others, I reclaim my energy, my confidence, and my peace. I am defined by my actions, my heart, and the love I give to myself and the world. I am proud of who I am, and that is enough.

Morning Prompt

How can you remain true to yourself today,
regardless of others' opinions?

_____

_____

_____

_____

_____

_____

_____

_____

_____

_____

_____

_____

_____

_____

_____

_____

_____

_____

_____

_____

Evening Prompt

Reflect on any moments today where others' opinions impacted you.
How can you release their influence?

_____

_____

_____

_____

_____

_____

_____

_____

_____

_____

_____

_____

_____

_____

_____

_____

_____

_____

_____

_____

_____

Day 28

"I bring value to the spaces I enter."

Every room I walk into is better because I am there. I carry with me unique gifts, insights, and energy that positively impact those around me. My presence alone adds meaning and depth to the spaces I occupy, and I am proud of the value I bring.

Whether it's through my words, actions, or simply the way I show up, I contribute something meaningful. I don't need to prove my worth or overextend myself to be valuable—my authenticity is enough. I trust that my ideas,

kindness, and perspective leave a lasting impression wherever I go.

Today, I will walk into every space with confidence, knowing that I have something special to offer. I will engage with intention and integrity, allowing my light to shine without hesitation. I will honor the ways I uplift, inspire, and support others, recognizing the ripple effect of my contributions.

By embracing the value I bring, I create connections and opportunities that align with my purpose. I am a force for positivity, growth, and change, and I am grateful for the impact I make. My presence matters, and the spaces I enter are enriched because I am there.

Morning Prompt

What unique qualities will you bring to your interactions today?

_____

_____

_____

_____

_____

_____

_____

_____

_____

_____

_____

_____

_____

_____

_____

_____

_____

_____

_____

_____

_____

_____

Evening Prompt

How did you show up with value in your spaces today?

_____

_____

_____

_____

_____

_____

_____

_____

_____

_____

_____

_____

_____

_____

_____

_____

_____

_____

_____

_____

_____

_____

_____

Day 29

"I am confident in my abilities and decisions."

I trust myself to make choices that align with my values, goals, and intuition. My abilities have been shaped by my experiences, knowledge, and growth, and I honor the hard work I've put into becoming the person I am today. I don't have to doubt myself because I know I am capable and prepared to handle whatever comes my way.

Confidence doesn't mean I'll always have all the answers—it means I trust my ability to figure things out. Even when faced with uncertainty, I believe in my capacity

to make decisions that serve my highest good. Every step I take reinforces my belief in myself and the path I've chosen.

Today, I will approach challenges and opportunities with self-assurance, knowing that I am equipped with the tools and wisdom to succeed. I will embrace my decisions without second-guessing, trusting that each one is a step toward my growth and fulfillment.

By being confident in my abilities and decisions, I create a foundation of trust and stability within myself. I am proud of the choices I make, the actions I take, and the person I am becoming. My confidence is my strength, and it empowers me to navigate life with clarity and courage.

Morning Prompt

What decision will you make today that requires self-trust?

_____

_____

_____

_____

_____

_____

_____

_____

_____

_____

_____

_____

_____

_____

_____

_____

_____

_____

_____

_____

_____

_____

Evening Prompt

Reflect on a decision you made today.
How did it affirm your confidence?

_____

_____

_____

_____

_____

_____

_____

_____

_____

_____

_____

_____

_____

_____

_____

_____

_____

_____

_____

_____

_____

Day 30

"I embrace who I am and know that I am more than enough."

I choose to fully accept and honor myself, just as I am. I let go of the need for external validation, knowing that my worth comes from within. I am a unique and valuable individual, and my presence makes a difference in this world. I don't need to change or prove anything to be enough—I already am.

Embracing who I am means loving both my strengths and my imperfections. It means celebrating my journey, the lessons I've learned, and the person I'm becoming. I trust

that I am exactly where I'm meant to be, and I have every-thing I need within me to thrive.

Today, I will stand confidently in my truth, reminding myself that I am more than enough. I will silence self-doubt and speak to myself with compassion and love. I will honor my worth by living authentically and unapolo-getically.

By embracing who I am, I create a life filled with self-love, empowerment, and joy. I am proud of the person I am, and I know that I bring unique value to the world. I am more than enough, and I carry this truth with confidence and grace.

Morning Prompt

*What will you remind yourself today to embrace
your enough-ness fully?*

_____

_____

_____

_____

_____

_____

_____

_____

_____

_____

_____

_____

_____

_____

_____

_____

_____

_____

_____

_____

_____

_____

Evening Prompt

How did you show yourself that you are enough today?

_____

_____

_____

_____

_____

_____

_____

_____

_____

_____

_____

_____

_____

_____

_____

_____

_____

_____

_____

_____

_____

_____

Gratitude

GRATITUDE

Introduction

Gratitude is one of the most grounding, healing, and heart-opening practices we can give to ourselves. It's more than just saying thank you—it's about fully feeling present in the moment and recognizing the beauty, joy, and lessons that life gives us every single day. It's the ability to pause and appreciate what you have before rushing toward what's next. Gratitude doesn't mean life is perfect. It means that even in the midst of chaos, change, or challenge, you're choosing to focus on what is still good, still working, and still worth celebrating.

For me, gratitude looks different each day. Some days, it's being thankful for the big things—my family, my sweet

golden retriever Bubba, my warm bed, and the people who support and pour into me. Other days, it's the so-called "small" things that feel the most powerful. Like the barista who made my chai latte just right, the way the light hits the flowers on my desk, or the quiet moment when I'm baking something in the kitchen and the aroma makes me feel safe. These moments are small in action, but they carry so much weight—they're peaceful, comforting, and bring me back to myself.

Gratitude, in many ways, is like savoring your favorite dessert. You don't just take one bite and forget it—you remember the experience. You remember the sweetness, the texture, the way it made you feel. You hold onto that moment even long after it's gone. That's what gratitude does for life. It teaches us to hold onto the good, to reflect on it in a way that brings warmth, peace, and even strength in difficult times. Because when you're grateful, you're not just noticing what's around you—you're feeling it, and those feelings stay with you long after the moment has passed.

Why Gratitude Matters

Gratitude shifts the way we see the world. Without it, we tend to focus on what's lacking—what we didn't get done, what went wrong, what we're still waiting for. But when we choose to practice gratitude, our mindset shifts from scarcity to abundance. We start to see life for what it is, rather than what it isn't. We realize how much goodness already surrounds us, and how even the smallest moments can carry deep meaning.

When we make gratitude a habit, we stop chasing happiness and begin experiencing it in real-time. It's not always easy—especially on the tough days when things feel heavy or when nothing seems to go right. But those are the days gratitude matters the most. It acts like an anchor, keeping us grounded when our emotions try to sweep us away. Gratitude reminds us that even in the middle of a rough season, there's still beauty to be found. A kind word. A moment of laughter. A good meal. A deep breath. A chance to try again.

Gratitude in Difficult Moments

I remember when I first tried keeping a gratitude journal. It wasn't easy—especially on the days when I was in a bad mood. I had a habit of letting one negative moment turn into a bad day. If one thing went wrong, I would spiral into everything that wasn't going right. And honestly? There are still days like that. But what I realized over time is that it wasn't just about writing gratitude—it was about living it.

If I wasn't taking in the good moments as they were happening, if I wasn't expressing my gratitude in real-time—whether that meant writing it down, saying it out loud, or simply pausing to breathe it in—I would miss it. I'd forget it. I'd let it slip away without letting it nourish me. And once those good moments were forgotten, the negative ones had more space to take over.

So I started practicing gratitude differently. I made it a discipline—not a chore, but a commitment. Whether I was driving and saw a beautiful sunset, sipping tea in silence, or getting a thoughtful text from someone I love, I'd stop and acknowledge it. Sometimes I'd write it in my notes app,

sometimes I'd speak it out loud in my room, sometimes I'd send someone a thank-you message just because. The more I practiced, the more my mind started shifting. Not because life got easier, but because I got better at seeing what was already good.

The Daily Practice of Gratitude

Now, I try to check in with myself every day. Not just at night when the day is done, but throughout the day—in little ways. I take time in the morning to appreciate the quiet, to reflect while I make breakfast, and again at night, when I give myself space to breathe and be present. These rituals have become part of my peace. Gratitude grounds me when I'm overwhelmed and helps me stay centered when everything else feels loud.

Some days, gratitude is loud and clear. Other days, it's quiet and hidden in the details. But it's always there. And by learning to look for it, I've trained my heart to feel more full—even when things aren't perfect. Gratitude is not about ignoring hard feelings; it's about making space for both the hard and the beautiful. It teaches us to hold both joy and struggle, and to choose presence over perfection.

How You Can Start Practicing Gratitude Today

If you're trying to build a gratitude practice, start with this: notice the moment while you're in it. When something brings you joy, pause. Let it land. Whether it's a smile from a stranger, a peaceful walk, or your favorite snack after a long day—pause and acknowledge it. Don't wait until the day is over to feel grateful for something that made you feel alive in the moment. Write it down, say it out loud, or reflect on it in silence—whatever feels right for you.

And don't worry if it feels forced at first. Gratitude, like any habit, takes time. But the more you practice, the more naturally it comes. You'll start to notice that your perspective shifts, your heart softens, and your days begin to feel fuller—not because they're suddenly perfect, but because you're finally noticing what's always been there.

Gratitude is a way of slowing down, of coming home to yourself. It helps you appreciate life while you're living it, not just in hindsight. Because the truth is—we never regret the moments we paused to be grateful. We only regret the ones we rushed through. So take your time. Savor your life like your favorite dessert. Let the sweetness stay with you. Gratitude isn't just a feeling—it's a way of being.

Day 31

"I am grateful for the abundance in my life."

Abundance surrounds me in countless ways, and today I choose to recognize and appreciate it. From the simple joys that brighten my day to the opportunities that allow me to grow, my life is filled with blessings. By focusing on gratitude, I open my heart to even more abundance.

Gratitude shifts my perspective, reminding me to celebrate what I have rather than dwell on what I lack. I acknowledge the love, connections, experiences, and resources that make my life rich and meaningful. Even in

moments of challenge, I can find something to be thankful for, knowing that each experience adds value to my journey.

Today, I will take a moment to reflect on the abundance in my life, big or small. I will express thanks for the people who support me, the opportunities I've been given, and the lessons I've learned. Gratitude doesn't just bring me peace—it attracts even more positivity and prosperity into my life.

By focusing on the abundance around me, I cultivate a mindset of joy and contentment. I am grateful for what I have, excited for what's to come, and confident that I am always surrounded by the infinite possibilities life has to offer.

Morning Prompt

List three things you're grateful for this morning.
How do they inspire you?

_____

_____

_____

_____

_____

_____

_____

_____

_____

_____

_____

_____

_____

_____

_____

_____

_____

_____

_____

_____

_____

Evening Prompt

What moments of abundance did you notice today, big or small?

_____

_____

_____

_____

_____

_____

_____

_____

_____

_____

_____

_____

_____

_____

_____

_____

_____

_____

_____

_____

Day 32

"I choose gratitude over comparison."

It's easy to get caught in the cycle of comparison, measuring my life against the highlight reels of others. But today, I choose a different path. I choose gratitude, knowing that my journey is unique and perfectly tailored for me. Instead of focusing on what I lack, I celebrate all that I have.

Gratitude shifts my perspective, reminding me to appreciate the blessings, opportunities, and growth I've experienced. It helps me see the beauty in my own story and frees me from the weight of comparison. I am not in com-

petition with anyone else—my only goal is to grow into the best version of myself.

Today, I will pause and acknowledge the things I am thankful for, big and small. I will focus on my strengths, my progress, and the moments of joy in my life. When comparison tries to creep in, I will gently redirect my thoughts to gratitude and appreciation for my journey.

By choosing gratitude, I embrace peace and contentment. I honor my own path while celebrating the successes of others, knowing that there is enough room for everyone to thrive. Gratitude fills my heart and allows me to live authentically and fully.

Morning Prompt

*How can you focus on gratitude instead of comparing
yourself to others today?*

Evening Prompt

Reflect on a moment today where you chose gratitude over comparison. How did it shift your mindset?

_____

_____

_____

_____

_____

_____

_____

_____

_____

_____

_____

_____

_____

_____

_____

_____

_____

_____

_____

_____

_____

Day 33

"I appreciate the beauty of small moments."

Life's most profound joys are often found in the little things—the warm sunlight on my face, the laughter of a loved one, the taste of my favorite dessert. These small moments might seem ordinary, but when I pause to notice them, I realize they are what make life extraordinary.

By appreciating these fleeting experiences, I ground myself in the present and invite gratitude into my day. Each small moment reminds me that joy doesn't have to come from grand events or big achievements. Happiness is

woven into the tiny details of everyday life, waiting to be noticed and cherished.

Today, I will slow down and be mindful of the beauty around me. I will take a deep breath and savor the small moments—a kind word, a comforting breeze, or the feeling of accomplishment after completing a task. These moments are gifts, and I choose to treasure them.

By embracing the beauty of small moments, I create a life filled with presence, gratitude, and wonder. These simple joys add depth and meaning to my days, reminding me that the greatest treasures are often found in the smallest things.

Morning Prompt

What small, beautiful moment can you look forward to experiencing today?

Evening Prompt

What small moment brought you joy or peace today?

Day 34

"I am thankful for how far I have come."

As I reflect on my journey, I am filled with gratitude for the progress I've made. Every step, no matter how big or small, has brought me closer to the person I am today. The challenges I've faced, the lessons I've learned, and the growth I've experienced are all testaments to my resilience and determination.

It's easy to focus on how far I still want to go, but today, I choose to celebrate how far I've already come. I honor the strength it took to overcome obstacles, the courage it

took to keep moving forward, and the perseverance that carried me through difficult times. My journey hasn't always been easy, but it has been meaningful.

Today, I will pause and appreciate my progress. I will give myself credit for the efforts I've made, the goals I've achieved, and the person I've become along the way. Gratitude for my journey fills me with confidence and hope for the future.

By being thankful for how far I've come, I remind myself that I am capable of continuing to grow and achieve. My past is proof of my strength, and my future is filled with possibility. I am proud of my journey, and I embrace it with gratitude and grace.

Morning Prompt

Reflect on a challenge you've overcome.
How does it inspire you today?

_____
_____
_____
_____
_____
_____
_____
_____
_____
_____
_____
_____
_____
_____
_____
_____
_____
_____
_____
_____
_____

Evening Prompt

What did you do today that reminded you of your growth journey?

_____

_____

_____

_____

_____

_____

_____

_____

_____

_____

_____

_____

_____

_____

_____

_____

_____

_____

_____

_____

_____

_____

Day 35

"Gratitude fills my heart and lights my path."

When I center myself in gratitude, everything around me becomes brighter. I recognize the abundance in my life, from the people who support me to the small moments of joy that bring peace to my day. Gratitude shifts my focus from what is missing to what is present, grounding me in the beauty of the here and now.

With a grateful heart, I find clarity and direction. Gratitude helps me see opportunities, appreciate the lessons in challenges, and approach life with optimism. It reminds me

that even in difficult times, there is something to be thankful for, something to guide me forward with hope.

Today, I will let gratitude be my guide. I will take a moment to reflect on the blessings in my life and allow them to fill my heart with warmth and peace. Each step I take, illuminated by gratitude, brings me closer to living a life of purpose and fulfillment.

By embracing gratitude, I align myself with joy, resilience, and abundance. It lights my path, showing me that even the smallest blessings have the power to transform my perspective and enrich my journey. Gratitude is my anchor and my light, and I carry it with me wherever I go.

Morning Prompt

How will you intentionally cultivate gratitude today?

Evening Prompt

What lit your path with gratitude today?

Healing

HEALING

Introduction

Healing is not a straight path—it's a layered, emotional, and deeply personal journey. It's not just about recovering from physical pain or getting past a difficult situation—it's about going within. It's about recognizing where you're still hurting, where you've been suppressing emotions, and where parts of you are asking to be seen, heard, and nurtured. Healing asks us to slow down and take an honest look at ourselves—not to shame or criticize, but to understand, accept, and grow. It requires bravery because sometimes facing what hurt us is more terrifying than what we're trying to move on from.

I didn't have a single moment where I knew, "This is

when I need to heal." But after my car accident, the days began to feel heavier. Sure, I was healing physically from a lower back injury, kidney trauma, and a concussion—but emotionally and mentally, I was unraveling. I didn't feel like myself. I didn't feel joy. And over time, I realized it wasn't just my body that needed rest—it was my mind and spirit. I started writing again. Writing what I was feeling, what I had been through, what I wanted my life to become. Not because I had the answers, but because I needed to give my pain somewhere to go. I needed to let it speak so I could begin to listen.

Why Healing Matters

Healing matters because we carry what we don't confront. It sits in our chest, our habits, our tone, our relationships—even in the way we talk to ourselves. When we avoid healing, we start reacting from wounds instead of responding from wisdom. We project, we overthink, we lash out, or we retreat completely—not because we don't care, but because we haven't yet learned how to care for ourselves in those moments of discomfort.

I started noticing this in my adult relationships and friendships. Certain things—certain words, tones, or situations—would trigger a reaction in me that didn't feel like the real me. I would retreat, shut down, or overthink everything someone did. And even when I tried to explain what I was feeling, I knew deep down that no one could fully take that weight off my shoulders. That weight was mine to carry, not because I deserved the pain, but because I needed to understand it. I needed to learn how not to put that emotional pressure on others, to stop self-sabotaging

relationships with fears that were rooted in past pain, not current truth.

Healing helped me realize that sometimes, the work isn't just for you—it's for the people around you too. Because when we don't heal, we pass on our pain. Unintentionally, but inevitably. And the cycle continues. But when we choose to heal, we break that cycle. We start showing up as someone more whole, more present, and more loving—not just for others, but for ourselves.

The Tools That Helped Me Heal

For me, writing has always been my greatest tool. It's where I feel safest. My journal holds the thoughts I didn't know how to say out loud. It's where my scattered feelings start to make sense. Writing feels like brain-dumping all the heaviness in my head and translating it into words that I can actually understand. It's like thinking a thought, but finally hearing it once you put it on paper. That's when things begin to connect.

I've also leaned into therapy and trusted conversations. Confiding in people who could hold space for me—without judgment—made a huge difference. Healing doesn't mean you have to do it alone. In fact, I believe healing invites you to let the right people in—those who guide, support, and uplift you, not those who try to fix you. Whether it's a counselor, a mentor, a friend, or even a supportive stranger, having someone witness your healing without trying to rush it is powerful.

The truth is, healing looks different for everyone. Sometimes it's crying it out. Sometimes it's sitting in silence. Sometimes it's laughing again after not feeling joy

for a while. Sometimes it's deleting the contact, blocking the number, unfollowing the account. Whatever it looks like, honor that version of healing. Don't compare your process to someone else's timeline.

How Healing Changed Me

Healing changed everything about how I view life, people, and myself. One of the biggest shifts I've noticed is how healing helped me detach—not from love or connection, but from people and patterns that no longer aligned with who I was becoming. As I started to heal deeper wounds, especially around my self-worth and people-pleasing, I noticed that some people who had been in my life for years were no longer meant to stay. And not because they were "bad," but because they were connected to an unhealed version of me.

Some of them fed off my insecurities, off my need to be liked, off my fear of confrontation. Once I started healing those parts of myself, the bond we had started to weaken. And while that was painful at first, I realized that it was necessary. Healing helped me walk away from what wasn't meant for me, so I could finally make space for the people, habits, and dreams that were. It gave me clarity. It gave me peace. And most of all, it gave me me—the version of myself I had buried under fear, doubt, and trauma.

Now, I walk through life with more self-trust, more patience, and more compassion—not just for others, but for myself. I no longer feel like I have to carry everything alone or suppress my emotions to be "strong." Strength is in softness too. And healing taught me that.

How You Can Begin Your Own Healing Journey

If you're holding on to pain that you haven't yet had the space or courage to face, I want you to know: you're not broken—you're just carrying too much. And it's okay to finally set it down. You don't have to heal all at once. Start with honesty. Ask yourself what moments still replay in your mind. What still triggers you? What still makes your heart feel heavy? These are invitations to heal, not to punish yourself—but to understand.

You can start small. Write it out. Cry if you need to. Seek help if it feels too heavy to hold alone. Healing isn't a one-time decision—it's a series of small acts of love that you choose to give yourself each day. And yes, some days it will feel like progress. Other days it might feel like a setback. But every step you take is still a step forward.

Healing isn't linear. It's messy, uncomfortable, and often painful. But it's also freeing, transformative, and powerful beyond words. It will teach you how to hold yourself better, how to show up in your relationships more fully, and how to live without carrying so much of your past on your shoulders. You deserve to experience life in a way that doesn't feel like survival. You deserve joy, softness, clarity, and peace. Let this be your gentle reminder that healing isn't about erasing your story—it's about rewriting how it continues.

Day 36

"I am healing, one day at a time."

Healing is not a race; it's a gentle process that unfolds in its own time. I remind myself that every day, no matter how small the steps, I am moving forward. Some days may feel heavier than others, but even on those days, I am still healing. My progress may not always be visible, but it is real and meaningful.

Each moment of self-care, every kind word I speak to myself, and every effort I make to prioritize my well-being is part of my healing journey. I allow myself the grace to feel, to rest, and to grow at my own pace. Healing is not

about perfection—it's about progress and learning to embrace each stage of the journey.

Today, I will honor my healing process. I will celebrate the small victories, such as a lighter heart, a clearer mind, or a single step forward. I will remind myself that healing is a sign of my strength and resilience, not my weakness.

By taking it one day at a time, I am creating space for renewal and growth. I trust in my ability to heal and become stronger, more balanced, and more at peace. My healing is a testament to my courage, and I am proud of the journey I am on.

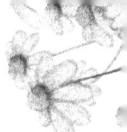

Morning Prompt

What part of your healing journey will you focus on today?

Evening Prompt

*Reflect on any healing moments or breakthroughs
you experienced today.*

_____

_____

_____

_____

_____

_____

_____

_____

_____

_____

_____

_____

_____

_____

_____

_____

_____

_____

_____

_____

_____

Day 37

"I release what no longer serves me."

Holding onto what no longer aligns with my growth can feel heavy, but I have the power to let go. Whether it's outdated beliefs, toxic relationships, past mistakes, or lingering fears, I release them with love and gratitude for the lessons they've taught me. By letting go, I make space for peace, clarity, and new opportunities.

Releasing doesn't mean forgetting—it means freeing myself from the weight of what is no longer meant for me. It's an act of self-care, a declaration that my well-being is a

priority. I trust that by letting go, I am creating room for better things to come.

Today, I will reflect on what no longer serves me and consciously choose to let it go. Whether it's through a deep breath, a journal entry, or a simple acknowledgment, I will release the ties that hold me back. I deserve a life filled with lightness, joy, and alignment.

By releasing what no longer serves me, I step into my power. I honor my journey and trust the process of renewal. My past has shaped me, but it does not define me. I am free to move forward, unburdened, and open to all the possibilities ahead.

Morning Prompt

What habit, thought, or relationship do you need to release today to grow?

_____

_____

_____

_____

_____

_____

_____

_____

_____

_____

_____

_____

_____

_____

_____

_____

_____

_____

_____

_____

_____

_____

_____

_____

_____

_____

Evening Prompt

Did you release anything today that held you back?
How do you feel now?

_____

_____

_____

_____

_____

_____

_____

_____

_____

_____

_____

_____

_____

_____

_____

_____

_____

_____

_____

_____

_____

Day 38

"My past does not define me; my present shapes my future."

I acknowledge my past as a part of my story, but it does not dictate who I am or where I am going. The choices I make today, the mindset I cultivate, and the actions I take are what shape my future. I have the power to create a life that aligns with my goals, dreams, and values.

My past has taught me lessons, shown me strength, and brought me to this moment. While I honor the journey that has led me here, I refuse to let past mistakes, challenges, or pain hold me back. I am not bound by what

was—I am empowered by what is and inspired by what can be.

Today, I will focus on the present, taking intentional steps toward the future I envision. I will release any lingering shame, regret, or doubt from my past and replace it with hope, gratitude, and determination. Each moment is an opportunity to grow, heal, and build a brighter tomorrow.

By grounding myself in the present, I reclaim my power. I am not a prisoner of my past—I am the architect of my future. With each decision I make, I move closer to becoming the person I aspire to be. My past does not define me; my present shapes my future, and my future is limitless.

Morning Prompt

How can you use today to build the future you desire?

Evening Prompt

Reflect on how your actions today shaped your present and future.

_____

_____

_____

_____

_____

_____

_____

_____

_____

_____

_____

_____

_____

_____

_____

_____

_____

_____

_____

_____

_____

Day 39

"I give myself permission to feel and let go."

Emotions are a natural and important part of my journey, and I honor them by allowing myself to feel fully. I give myself permission to sit with my feelings—whether they are joy, sadness, anger, or fear—without judgment. By acknowledging my emotions, I create space for healing and release.

Letting go doesn't mean ignoring or suppressing how I feel; it means processing my emotions and then freeing myself from the weight they may carry. I understand that

holding onto pain, resentment, or worry only limits my growth and peace. Releasing them is an act of self-love and liberation.

Today, I will give myself the grace to feel without rushing or pressuring myself to move on too quickly. I will find healthy ways to express and process my emotions, such as journaling, meditating, or talking to someone I trust. Once I've allowed myself to feel, I will gently let go of what no longer serves me.

By feeling and letting go, I free myself to embrace the present moment and move forward with clarity and lightness. I trust that releasing the old makes room for the new—new experiences, new joys, and new opportunities. I give myself permission to heal, to grow, and to let go.

Morning Prompt

What emotions or experiences need your attention today?
How will you honor them?

_____

_____

_____

_____

_____

_____

_____

_____

_____

_____

_____

_____

_____

_____

_____

_____

_____

_____

_____

_____

_____

_____

Evening Prompt

What did you let go of today, and how did it bring you peace?

_____

_____

_____

_____

_____

_____

_____

_____

_____

_____

_____

_____

_____

_____

_____

_____

_____

_____

_____

_____

Day 40

"My healing is my priority."

I am worthy of the time, care, and effort it takes to heal. My well-being is not something to be placed on the back-burner—it is essential to living a balanced and fulfilling life. By prioritizing my healing, I am showing myself the love and respect I deserve.

Healing doesn't happen overnight, and that's okay. It's a journey, and each small step I take matters. Whether it's seeking support, practicing self-care, or simply resting when I need to, every act of prioritizing my healing brings me closer to wholeness. I remind myself that this process

is not linear, but every moment of effort contributes to my growth.

Today, I will make space for my healing, honoring my needs without guilt or hesitation. I will set boundaries to protect my energy and say no to anything that hinders my progress. My healing is not selfish—it's necessary for me to show up fully for myself and the people I care about.

By making my healing a priority, I am building a strong foundation for my future. I am reclaiming my peace, my strength, and my joy. This is my time to heal, and I will embrace the journey with patience, compassion, and love.

Morning Prompt

How can you prioritize your healing today?

_____

_____

_____

_____

_____

_____

_____

_____

_____

_____

_____

_____

_____

_____

_____

_____

_____

_____

_____

_____

_____

Evening Prompt

*What healing practices or moments brought you
closer to wholeness today?*

_____

_____

_____

_____

_____

_____

_____

_____

_____

_____

_____

_____

_____

_____

_____

_____

_____

_____

_____

_____

Empowerment

EMPOWERMENT

Introduction

Empowerment is the moment you realize you are not just surviving—you are growing, blooming, and choosing your direction, even when the world tries to decide it for you. It's not about having all the answers or always being confident. It's about being rooted in who you are and choosing to keep showing up, even when the path is unclear. Empowerment is the courage to make decisions for yourself, the strength to stand tall in your truth, and the desire to uplift others while doing it. Like a flower breaking through the soil, it's a quiet yet powerful force that reminds you of your ability to rise.

Real empowerment doesn't always come from loud

declarations—it often starts in everyday moments. It's choosing to walk away from a conversation that drains you. It's asking for help when you're used to doing everything alone. It's saying "no" when you've been taught to always say "yes." Empowerment is being in control of your growth. And just like a garden needs light, nourishment, and space to breathe, we need the right environment, support, and tools to feel empowered. That's where my story begins—being surrounded by the kind of love that didn't just hold me but lifted me.

My Roots of Empowerment

I was fortunate to grow up in a household where I felt empowered—where my family believed in me, encouraged me, and reminded me that I had everything I needed to succeed already within me. They poured into me consistently, with words of affirmation, guidance, resources, and above all—unwavering support. And outside of my home, I had mentors who saw my potential before I did. They didn't just cheer for me—they challenged me, inspired me, and helped me bloom in ways I never thought possible.

Through their encouragement, I found my way into self-care work. I started speaking to students, sharing my story, writing books, and creating a space where people could come as they are and still feel whole. A space where self-care isn't just about bubble baths and break days—it's about healing, setting boundaries, building confidence, and learning to blossom again after you've been uprooted by life.

I started to understand that empowerment isn't something we keep for ourselves—it's something we pass on.

Empowerment, to me, is a domino effect. When one person is empowered, they begin to empower everyone around them. It becomes a chain of light—lighting up one person at a time. That's why who you surround yourself with matters. You need people who pour into your soul as much as you pour into theirs. People who want to see you win. People who will hold the mirror up to remind you of your power when you forget.

What Empowerment Looks Like in Real Life

Empowerment isn't always some big, bold transformation. Sometimes it's subtle—but strong. It's choosing yourself after years of putting others first. It's standing firm in a decision that aligns with your peace. It's creating something meaningful and knowing that you don't need anyone's permission to do so. For me, it was saying yes to myself—yes to writing my truth, yes to speaking to students about their value, yes to creating a space for people to feel seen.

One of the most empowering moments of my life wasn't just about taking control—it was about choosing to believe I was worthy of that control. I had to learn how to lead myself before I could guide others. I had to trust that even though I didn't have everything figured out, I still had something valuable to give. And from there, everything began to grow.

The more I empowered myself, the more I saw how others blossomed in my presence—not because I had all the answers, but because I held space for them to find their own. That's what empowerment is—it's not about being

above others. It's about walking beside them with your light on, so they remember they can shine too.

How Empowering Myself Helped Me Empower Others

I didn't walk through my healing or growth journey alone—and I don't pretend to. I had people who showed up for me, who reminded me of my worth when I felt small, who poured into me when I was running low. And that reflection has become my mission: to be that light for someone else. To pour into others, to share my story, my resources, my knowledge—without holding back, without dimming someone else's light just to keep mine shining.

Empowerment taught me that lifting others up doesn't take anything away from you. In fact, it multiplies your strength. It creates space for everyone to bloom. I now understand that my ability to stand tall and speak up isn't just a gift for me—it's an invitation for others to do the same. That's why I write, why I speak, and why I show up—because I know how much it meant for me to have someone believe in me, and I want to be that for someone else.

Whether you're starting your journey or are already blooming into your power, know this: empowerment isn't about perfection—it's about progression. It's about choosing yourself. And when you do that, you create space for others to choose themselves too.

How You Can Start Cultivating Empowerment Today

Empowerment begins with permission—the permission to be fully you. You don't need to wait for a title, a milestone, or a round of applause. You are already enough to start. Begin by rooting yourself in truth. What do you want? What brings you joy? What would your life look like if you stopped holding yourself back?

Then nourish your growth. Spend time with people who uplift you. Journal your dreams, even the scary ones. Practice saying "no" without guilt and "yes" without fear. Speak life into yourself the same way you speak it into your friends. And most importantly—when you feel strong, share that strength. Empowerment is contagious. When you water your own garden, you naturally inspire others to do the same.

You are not here to dim your light. You are here to shine so brightly that others remember they can too. Let your story be proof that when you are rooted in your truth, you will always find your way back to yourself—and bloom, again and again.

Day 41

"I am capable of achieving my dreams."

My dreams are not just distant possibilities—they are attainable goals within my reach. I have the skills, determination, and resilience needed to bring them to life. Every step I take, no matter how small, moves me closer to the future I envision for myself.

Achieving my dreams requires effort, but I am not afraid of hard work. I trust in my ability to overcome challenges and adapt to whatever comes my way. My belief in myself fuels my actions, and I know that with

persistence and focus, I can accomplish anything I set my mind to.

Today, I will take intentional steps toward my dreams, no matter how big or small. I will celebrate my progress and remind myself that I am worthy of success and fulfillment. I will not let fear, doubt, or setbacks discourage me because I know they are simply part of the journey.

By affirming my capability, I align my mindset with my goals and open the door to endless possibilities. I am confident, determined, and unstoppable. My dreams are within my grasp, and I am capable of achieving them with grace, strength, and perseverance.

Morning Prompt

What dream will you take a step toward today,
no matter how small?

Evening Prompt

Reflect on any actions or thoughts that
aligned with your dreams today.

_____

_____

_____

_____

_____

_____

_____

_____

_____

_____

_____

_____

_____

_____

_____

_____

_____

_____

_____

_____

_____

_____

Day 42

"I am the creator of my reality."

My thoughts, actions, and choices shape the life I live. I hold the power to create a reality that aligns with my dreams, values, and purpose. By focusing on positivity, taking intentional steps, and believing in my potential, I can turn my vision into my reality.

Every day is an opportunity to make choices that reflect the life I desire. I am not a passive observer in my journey—I am an active participant, capable of influencing my circumstances and outcomes. Even when

faced with challenges, I have the power to shift my perspective and find a way forward.

Today, I will take ownership of my life, knowing that I have the ability to create the reality I want. I will act with intention, embrace opportunities, and trust in my capacity to manifest my goals. My mindset, effort, and belief in myself are the foundation of my success.

By embracing my role as the creator of my reality, I empower myself to dream boldly and act decisively. I am not limited by fear or doubt—I am guided by purpose and determination. My life is a canvas, and I am painting it with the colors of my choosing.

Morning Prompt

What reality are you building today?
How can you actively shape it?

Evening Prompt

What did you do today to create the life you want?

_____

_____

_____

_____

_____

_____

_____

_____

_____

_____

_____

_____

_____

_____

_____

_____

_____

_____

_____

_____

Day 43

"I choose to empower myself through action."

Empowerment comes from within, and I recognize that my choices and actions have the power to shape my life. By taking intentional steps forward, no matter how small, I remind myself of my strength and capability. I refuse to remain still, knowing that even the smallest effort can lead to meaningful progress.

Every action I take is a declaration of my belief in myself. I choose to act with courage, even when I feel uncertain because I trust in my ability to learn, grow, and

adapt. I know that waiting for the "perfect moment" only delays my progress; instead, I create momentum through consistent, purposeful action.

Today, I will take one step toward my goals, no matter how challenging they may seem. I will embrace the discomfort of growth, understanding that empowerment comes from doing, not just dreaming. Each action I take strengthens my confidence and brings me closer to the life I desire.

By choosing action, I reclaim my power and remind myself that I am in control of my journey. I am capable, resilient, and unstoppable. Through action, I empower myself to turn possibilities into realities.

Morning Prompt

What empowering action will you take today?

_____

_____

_____

_____

_____

_____

_____

_____

_____

_____

_____

_____

_____

_____

_____

_____

_____

_____

_____

_____

_____

_____

Evening Prompt

How did today's actions empower you?
What did you learn about your strength?

_____

_____

_____

_____

_____

_____

_____

_____

_____

_____

_____

_____

_____

_____

_____

_____

_____

_____

_____

_____

_____

_____

_____

Day 44

"I have everything I need within me to succeed."

Success begins with the belief that I am already equipped with the tools, talents, and resilience necessary to achieve my goals. My experiences have shaped me, my determination fuels me, and my inner strength guides me. I don't need to seek validation or approval from the outside world—I trust in my own abilities.

I remind myself that challenges are not barriers but opportunities to unlock my potential. Every skill I've developed, every lesson I've learned, and every step I've

taken has prepared me for this moment. I have the creativity, problem-solving ability, and perseverance needed to navigate any obstacle.

Today, I will approach my goals with confidence, knowing that I am capable of finding solutions and adapting when needed. I will trust my intuition and make decisions that align with my purpose. With each effort I make, I am building the foundation for my success.

By affirming that I have everything I need within me, I embrace a mindset of self-reliance and empowerment. I am strong, capable, and resourceful, and I trust that my inner resources will lead me to the success I envision.

Morning Prompt

What inner resource will you lean on today to achieve your goals?

Evening Prompt

How did your inner strength or resources help you succeed today?

_____

_____

_____

_____

_____

_____

_____

_____

_____

_____

_____

_____

_____

_____

_____

_____

_____

_____

_____

_____

_____

_____

Day 45

"I am the creator of my reality."

It takes courage to embrace and express who I truly am. In a world that often encourages conformity, I choose to honor my authenticity. I remind myself that my uniqueness is my strength, and the most powerful thing I can do is show up as my true self, unapologetically.

Being myself doesn't mean I'll never face judgment or misunderstanding, but I know that I am not defined by others' opinions. I am worthy of love, respect, and belonging just as I am. By embracing my individuality, I inspire others to do the same, creating connections that are genuine and meaningful.

Today, I will stand tall in my truth, letting go of the fear of rejection or judgment. I will show up with confidence, vulnerability, and integrity, knowing that who I am is enough. I will celebrate the qualities that make me different and use them as a source of strength.

By being brave enough to show up as myself, I reclaim my power and align with my purpose. I trust that being true to who I am will open doors to opportunities, relationships, and experiences that are meant for me. My authenticity is my superpower, and I am proud to live it fully.

Morning Prompt

How will you show up authentically today?

Evening Prompt

When did you show courage in being yourself today?
How did it feel?

_____

_____

_____

_____

_____

_____

_____

_____

_____

_____

_____

_____

_____

_____

_____

_____

_____

_____

_____

Mindfulness

MINDFULNESS

Introduction

Mindfulness is the practice of being fully present in the moment—not stuck in the past, not worrying about the future, but grounded right where you are. It's about tuning in to your breath, your thoughts, your feelings, and your surroundings without judgment. It's about slowing down enough to notice the beauty of a blooming flower, the warmth of your tea cup, or the rhythm of your own heart-beat. In a world that constantly pushes us to do more, achieve more, and move faster, mindfulness invites us to pause, breathe, and be.

When I first discovered mindfulness, I wasn't seeking it for myself—I was helping with a program for kids. A guest facilitator came in and led them through a mindfulness session. She spoke to them about their emotions, thoughts, and how to manage both through mindful meditation. I joined in, thinking I was just helping facilitate—but something about the practice resonated deeply with me. Sitting still, focusing on my breath, and being aware of my emotions without judging them…it felt like I was watering a part of me I had neglected. That day planted the seed, and over time, mindfulness became one of the strongest roots in my journey of self-care.

Why Mindfulness Matters

Mindfulness brings us back to ourselves. It creates space between what we feel and how we react. It teaches us that we are not our thoughts—we are the observers of them. And when we begin to observe rather than absorb, we open ourselves up to understanding, peace, and clarity. In moments of stress or chaos, mindfulness doesn't make the storm disappear—it simply gives us the tools to find stillness within it.

Mindfulness allows us to bloom with intention. Instead of rushing through life, it helps us savor each step of the journey. It's in the way you close your eyes and focus on your breathing in the morning before facing the day. It's in the moment you choose to listen without interrupting, to respond with compassion rather than react with frustration. It's in noticing the colors of the sky at sunset, the way sunlight hits your window, or the weight of your body grounding into the earth during meditation.

Like a garden, your mind needs tending. Mindfulness is that gentle care—it's the watering, the pruning, the pa-

tience. It teaches you how to nourish your mind and emotions so you can grow in awareness and emotional
strength.

How Mindfulness Changed My Perspective

Practicing mindfulness daily—even if just for a min-
ute—has helped me stay rooted, especially in high-stress
situations. In the morning and again before I sleep, I take
time to ground myself. I do mindful meditation focused on
my breath, my thoughts, and my intentions. I remind myself to be kind. I practice non-judgment—not just toward
others, but toward myself. On hard days, that simple act of
giving myself grace can make all the difference. It keeps
me calm, observant, and connected, even when life feels
overwhelming.

There have been moments when everything around me
felt chaotic. Emotions running high, misunderstandings
piling up, tension so thick it could cut through peace like a
knife. Before I learned mindfulness, I might have added
fuel to that fire—reacting out of stress or anger. But now,
mindfulness gives me the pause I need. I stop. I breathe. I
observe what's going on outside of me and within me. I
ask myself, What am I feeling? What am I telling myself?
How can I respond with calm instead of chaos?

Mindfulness doesn't erase the emotions—it validates
them. But it also gently redirects me back to center, helping
me respond in ways that align with who I want to be.

The Blossoming Power of Presence

Mindfulness has helped me bloom from the inside out. I've become more in tune with my needs, more compassionate toward myself, and more intentional with my relationships. I've learned to notice when I'm slipping into old patterns—people-pleasing, overthinking, emotional spirals—and instead of spiraling deeper, I pause. I choose curiosity over criticism. I choose softness over shame.

This practice has not only helped me grow—but also helped me nurture the spaces I exist in. I've been able to be more present with others, to listen more deeply, and to respond more lovingly. It's changed how I show up for myself and for the people I care about. Because when you're rooted in mindfulness, you don't just react to life—you respond to it. With presence. With clarity. With peace.

How You Can Start Practicing Mindfulness Today

Let mindfulness become your inner garden—the place you return to when the world feels overwhelming and you need a moment to breathe. You don't have to wait for the perfect time, the perfect silence, or the perfect mindset to begin. Start where you are, with what you have. Maybe it's one quiet breath before you pick up your phone in the morning. Maybe it's savoring the warmth of your tea or the color of the sky outside your window. Maybe it's catching yourself in a spiral of overthinking and gently guiding yourself back with compassion instead of shame.

These small, present moments are not insignificant—

they are seeds. Every time you pause and acknowledge what you feel, every time you choose to respond with intention instead of reaction, you're planting something within yourself. Over time, these seeds of awareness blossom into clarity, self-trust, and emotional resilience. You begin to feel more rooted in who you are, less shaken by what's outside of your control.

Mindfulness is not about escaping life—it's about meeting it as it is. It's about returning home to yourself in a way that feels peaceful, grounded, and whole. When you practice mindfulness, you learn to carry peace with you wherever you go—not because life gets easier, but because you get stronger, more present, and more attuned to your inner light. You bloom, not in spite of the chaos—but through it. And that is the quiet, transformative power of mindfulness.

Day 46

"I am present in this moment."

This moment is a gift, and I choose to be fully here, embracing it with my whole heart. By letting go of the past and releasing worry about the future, I allow myself to experience the beauty and peace of the present. This is where life unfolds, where I can feel grounded and connected.

When I am present, I notice the little things—the sound of my breath, the way the sunlight dances through the window, the warmth of a smile. I find clarity and calm by simply being, without the need to rush or achieve. The present moment is enough, and so am I.

Today, I will gently bring my attention back to the now whenever my mind starts to wander. Through mindful breaths, focused attention, or moments of gratitude, I will anchor myself to this moment. This is where my power lies.

By being present, I open myself to joy, peace, and connection. I am not defined by what has passed or what is yet to come—I am here, and that is enough. In this moment, I find balance, gratitude, and the freedom to simply be.

Morning Prompt

What will you do today to remain present and mindful?

Evening Prompt

Reflect on a moment where you stayed present today.
How did it impact you?

_____

_____

_____

_____

_____

_____

_____

_____

_____

_____

_____

_____

_____

_____

_____

_____

_____

_____

_____

Day 47

"My breath is a source of calm and strength."

In moments of chaos or uncertainty, I turn to my breath as a steady, grounding force. Each inhale fills me with calm, and each exhale releases tension and worry. My breath is a constant companion, always available to center and support me.

By focusing on my breath, I connect to the present moment and remind myself of my inner strength. With every slow, intentional breath, I create space for peace and clarity to flow through me. My breath is a reminder that I have the power to calm my mind and body, no matter the circumstances.

Today, I will take moments to pause and breathe deeply, allowing my breath to guide me back to a place of balance and resilience. Whether I'm feeling overwhelmed, uncertain, or simply in need of a pause, I will trust in the soothing and empowering energy of my breath.

My breath is more than just a function—it is a source of life, calm, and strength. Through my breath, I reclaim my power and find the courage to face whatever comes my way. With each breath, I grow stronger, steadier, and more at peace.

Morning Prompt

How can you use your breath to guide you through today's challenges?

Evening Prompt

When did focusing on your breath bring you peace today?

_____

_____

_____

_____

_____

_____

_____

_____

_____

_____

_____

_____

_____

_____

_____

_____

_____

_____

_____

Day 48

**"I choose to respond with intention,
not react with emotion."**

In moments of challenge or conflict, I remind myself that I have the power to pause and choose my response. Reacting impulsively often leads to regret or misunderstanding, but responding with intention allows me to stay aligned with my values and maintain my peace.

By taking a moment to breathe and reflect, I create space to understand the situation and my emotions. I honor my feelings without letting them control my actions. This intentional approach empowers me to communicate clearly, set boundaries, and handle challenges with grace and clarity.

Today, I will practice mindfulness in my interactions, choosing responses that reflect who I want to be rather than reacting out of frustration or impulse. I will embrace patience, kindness, and understanding as tools to navigate even the most difficult moments.

By responding with intention, I strengthen my relationships and preserve my inner calm. I trust in my ability to act thoughtfully and stay true to myself, no matter the situation. My intentional responses create a life filled with harmony, respect, and self-control.

Morning Prompt

How can you pause and respond intentionally today?

_____

_____

_____

_____

_____

_____

_____

_____

_____

_____

_____

_____

_____

_____

_____

_____

_____

_____

_____

_____

Evening Prompt

Reflect on a moment where you responded with intention today.
How did it feel?

Day 49

"I am connected to the present and grounded in my truth."

In this moment, I feel deeply connected to the here and now, fully present in my body, mind, and spirit. By letting go of distractions and worries, I allow myself to embrace the clarity and peace of this moment. This connection to the present anchors me and reminds me of my strength.

Being grounded in my truth means honoring who I am and living authentically. I trust my inner voice and stand firm in my values, even when the world around me feels uncertain. My truth is my foundation, and it gives me the confidence to move through life with purpose and integrity.

Today, I will take time to ground myself, whether through mindful breathing, a walk in nature, or moments of stillness. I will listen to my inner wisdom and act in ways that align with my true self. This connection to the present moment strengthens my ability to live authentically and confidently.

By staying connected to the present and grounded in my truth, I find balance, clarity, and peace. I am unshaken by external noise because I trust in the power of my truth and the stability it brings. This is where I find my center, my strength, and my joy.

Morning Prompt

*What will help you stay grounded and aligned
with your truth today?*

_____

_____

_____

_____

_____

_____

_____

_____

_____

_____

_____

_____

_____

_____

_____

_____

_____

_____

_____

_____

_____

_____

Evening Prompt

*How did staying connected to your truth shape
your experiences today?*

_____

_____

_____

_____

_____

_____

_____

_____

_____

_____

_____

_____

_____

_____

_____

_____

_____

_____

_____

_____

_____

_____

Day 50

I honor my needs by slowing down when necessary.

Life can feel fast-paced and demanding, but I remind myself that it's okay to pause. Slowing down is not a sign of weakness—it's an act of self-respect and care. By listening to my body and mind, I honor my needs and create space to recharge and realign with what matters most.

When I slow down, I give myself the opportunity to rest, reflect, and reconnect. I let go of the pressure to constantly do more and embrace the value of simply being.

Slowing down allows me to be more present, intentional, and mindful in my actions.

Today, I will pay attention to the signals my body and emotions send me. If I feel tired, overwhelmed, or disconnected, I will give myself permission to pause without guilt. Whether it's taking a deep breath, stepping away from a task, or enjoying a moment of stillness, I will prioritize my well-being.

By honoring my needs and slowing down when necessary, I nurture my resilience and protect my peace. I trust that rest and reflection are just as important as action and progress. Slowing down isn't stopping—it's preparing myself to move forward with clarity, strength, and intention.

Morning Prompt

What pace do you need today to honor your well-being?

_____

_____

_____

_____

_____

_____

_____

_____

_____

_____

_____

_____

_____

_____

_____

_____

_____

_____

_____

Evening Prompt

Reflect on how slowing down (or not) impacted your day.

_____

_____

_____

_____

_____

_____

_____

_____

_____

_____

_____

_____

_____

_____

_____

_____

_____

_____

_____

_____

Abundance

ABUNDANCE

Introduction

Abundance is a word we hear often—but it's also one of the most misunderstood. It's easy to associate it with material things: overflowing bank accounts, luxury vacations, cars, designer clothes, or even popularity and status. But true abundance goes far beyond what we can touch, spend, or show off. Real abundance is a feeling. It's the deep-rooted sense that you are whole, worthy, and richly blessed—not because of what you have, but because of who you are and what lives inside you.

To me, abundance is being full of love, knowledge, peace, joy, and deep connection. It's the feeling of being surrounded by people who uplift your spirit. It's knowing that even if the world around you feels chaotic, there is still beauty in the simple things—the stillness of morning, the warmth of your pet curled beside you, the calm in your own breath. Abundance lives in the unseen. In the emotions you feel. In the kindness you offer. In the way you make people feel safe, seen, and understood.

Growing up, I witnessed abundance take on many different forms. Some people in my life defined it by how much money they had, what they wore, or what they could buy. Others defined it by how full their hearts were—by how present they were with their families, how open they were to learning, and how deeply they cared for the people around them. And while I respect everyone's personal definitions, I was always drawn to the ones who led with emotional wealth—the ones who bloomed from the inside out.

I began to notice that the people who chased self-fulfillment, who invested in their emotional well-being, who practiced gratitude and empathy, were often the most grounded and joyful. They were also the most generous— not just with money, but with time, attention, love, and wisdom. They lived richly not because of what they owned, but because of how they lived. And that changed the way I started to view abundance for myself. I no longer wanted to measure my life by what I could collect—I wanted to measure it by what I could give, grow, and feel.

The Shift From Scarcity to Blooming Abundance

There have been moments in my life where I didn't feel full—I felt like I was lacking something, even when I had

a lot. I would compare myself to others and feel behind. Like I wasn't doing enough, achieving enough, or becoming enough. I felt this silent pressure to keep chasing the next thing that would "prove" I was successful or worthy. But that mindset—what we call a scarcity mindset—is like planting a flower in dry soil. No matter how much you water it from the outside, it won't bloom if the roots are starved of nourishment.

I realized I had to shift my focus inward. I had to stop looking at what I didn't have and start recognizing the incredible blessings I was already surrounded by. My family. My faith. My dog Bubba, who brings me so much comfort. The fact that I can sit down and write, reflect, and share my truth. The people who support and pour into me. The ability to impact someone's life just by sharing my own story.

These are things that money can't buy. And when I began to see them as abundance, everything started to shift.

It's not that I stopped having goals or dreams. I still dream big, and I believe in success. But now, I pursue those dreams from a place of wholeness, not lack. I no longer need achievements to define my worth. I know that I'm already rooted in enoughness—and from that rich soil, everything else can bloom.

How I Practice Abundance in Everyday Life

Abundance, for me, starts with presence. It's a mindset. A practice. A lifestyle. I begin and end my days with gratitude—not just a list of things I'm thankful for, but a real pause to feel the depth of that gratitude. I reflect on the resources I've been blessed with, the growth I've experi-

enced, the people who pour into me. I practice mindfulness and self-compassion. I celebrate my wins, even the small ones. I let myself feel joy without guilt.

But abundance also lives in the way I treat others. I choose to speak with kindness, listen with care, and offer grace—not just when it's easy, but especially when it's hard. I give my time, my energy, my wisdom, and my encouragement freely, knowing that what I give is never truly lost—it always comes back, sometimes in unexpected ways.

To me, a truly abundant life is one where I can walk into a room and bring light with me. One where I help others believe in themselves just by believing in my own power. I look at the richness in my relationships, the depth of my self-awareness, the gentleness I've learned to offer my younger self—and I know, this is wealth. This is the kind of abundance that can't be taken away.

Letting Abundance Bloom in Your Life

If you're in a season where everything feels like "not enough"—I want you to pause and take a breath. I want you to look again, not at what's missing, but at what's already here. The fullness of your heart. The dreams inside your mind. The strength in your bones. The kindness in your voice. You have more than you think, and you are more than you've been told.

Start small. Let yourself feel joy in the little things—the way the sun hits your skin, the song that reminds you of a beautiful memory, the way someone's eyes light up when they talk about something they love. Let yourself be overwhelmed with gratitude for the present moment. Remind yourself that you don't need more to feel more. You need to see more of what's already within and around you.

Choose to bloom in your own time. Let your life unfold like a garden that needs time, space, and care. Tend to your thoughts like petals—remove the weeds of comparison, and water your roots with kindness. Trust that the more you lean into gratitude, the more abundance you'll begin to feel. Not because your life is perfect, but because you've stopped rushing and started receiving.

You were never meant to live in scarcity. You were meant to flourish. You were meant to be full—of peace, of purpose, of love. Let abundance be the lens you see life through. Let it remind you that there's always more beauty when you look with eyes of gratitude. And when you start living from that place of fullness, you'll not only bloom—you'll inspire everything around you to blossom too.

Day 51

"I am open to receiving all the abundance life offers."

Abundance surrounds me in countless forms—love, opportunities, joy, and growth. I remind myself that I am deserving of all the good that life has to offer. By opening my heart and mind, I create space to welcome abundance into my life without hesitation or doubt.

Being open to abundance means releasing limiting beliefs and trusting that there is more than enough to go around. I let go of fear, scarcity, and self-doubt, knowing that abundance flows freely when I align with gratitude and positivity. I am ready to receive the blessings that are meant for me.

Today, I will approach life with a sense of openness and trust. I will notice the gifts, big and small, that the universe places in my path. Whether it's a kind word, an unexpected opportunity, or a moment of peace, I will embrace abundance with gratitude and grace.

By staying open to abundance, I invite prosperity, joy, and love into my life. I am worthy of living a life filled with richness in all forms, and I trust that life will continue to provide in beautiful and unexpected ways. My openness allows abundance to flow effortlessly into my experience.

Morning Prompt

What abundance are you open to receiving today?

Evening Prompt

*What abundance did you notice or receive today,
and how did it feel?*

_____

_____

_____

_____

_____

_____

_____

_____

_____

_____

_____

_____

_____

_____

_____

_____

_____

_____

_____

_____

_____

_____

_____

Day 52

"I let go of limitations and welcome abundance into my life."

I release the thoughts, beliefs, and fears that have held me back. They no longer serve me or align with the person I am becoming. By letting go of these limitations, I create space for new opportunities, growth, and infinite possibilities. I trust that abundance is my natural state and that it flows to me with ease.

Welcoming abundance means shifting my mindset from scarcity to gratitude. I open my heart and mind to receive the blessings life has to offer, knowing there is more than enough for everyone, including me. With every step I take, I align myself with the energy of abundance and prosperity.

Today, I will recognize the abundance already present in my life and welcome even more with confidence and gratitude. I will take inspired action toward my goals, knowing that the universe supports me. I let go of self-doubt and embrace the limitless potential within me.

By releasing limitations and welcoming abundance, I step into a life of joy, success, and fulfillment. I trust that abundance flows freely to me, and I am ready to receive it in all its forms—with an open heart and a grateful spirit.

Morning Prompt

How will you approach today with a mindset of possibility?

_____

_____

_____

_____

_____

_____

_____

_____

_____

_____

_____

_____

_____

_____

_____

_____

_____

_____

_____

Evening Prompt

*Reflect on a moment where you embraced abundance
instead of scarcity today.*

Day 53

"I am grateful for the opportunities coming my way."

Every day brings new opportunities for growth, learning, and success. I may not always see them immediately, but I trust that they are unfolding in perfect timing. My gratitude for these opportunities opens my heart and mind to recognize and embrace them when they arrive.

By expressing gratitude, I align myself with positivity and abundance. This mindset allows me to approach opportunities with confidence and excitement, knowing

that each one is a chance to move closer to my goals and dreams. I am grateful for the lessons, connections, and experiences that every opportunity brings.

Today, I will focus on the possibilities around me, big and small. I will remain open and receptive, trusting that what is meant for me will find its way to me. Gratitude fills me with anticipation and joy for the opportunities yet to come.

By being thankful for the opportunities coming my way, I attract even more abundance and possibility into my life. I trust that the universe is working in my favor, and I am ready to embrace each opportunity with gratitude, courage, and enthusiasm.

Morning Prompt

What opportunity excites you today, and how can you make the most of it?

_____

_____

_____

_____

_____

_____

_____

_____

_____

_____

_____

_____

_____

_____

_____

_____

_____

_____

_____

_____

Evening Prompt

Did you recognize any opportunities today?
How did you embrace them?

_____

_____

_____

_____

_____

_____

_____

_____

_____

_____

_____

_____

_____

_____

_____

_____

_____

_____

_____

_____

_____

_____

Day 54

"Prosperity flows to me with ease and joy."

I am open to the abundance and prosperity that life has to offer. With every thought, action, and intention, I align myself with the flow of wealth, success, and joy. Prosperity is not something I have to chase—it is a natural part of who I am, and I welcome it into my life with gratitude and trust.

I release any resistance or doubt that may block the flow of prosperity. I deserve a life filled with ease, joy, and abundance. As I focus on positivity and gratitude, I attract

opportunities and resources that support my dreams and goals. Prosperity flows effortlessly when I trust in the process and remain open to receiving.

Today, I will embrace each moment with a prosperous mindset. I will celebrate the abundance already present in my life and look forward to the new blessings that are on their way. With every step I take, I affirm that prosperity is all around me.

By allowing prosperity to flow to me with ease and joy, I create a life of balance, fulfillment, and abundance. I trust that everything I need is on its way, and I am ready to receive it with open arms and a grateful heart.

Morning Prompt

How will you open yourself to prosperity today?

Evening Prompt

Reflect on how prosperity showed up for you today,
even in small ways.

_____

_____

_____

_____

_____

_____

_____

_____

_____

_____

_____

_____

_____

_____

_____

_____

_____

_____

Day 55

"I am open to receiving the infinite blessings life has to offer."

Life is abundant, and I trust that it has so much to give. I open my heart and mind to receive these blessings with gratitude and joy. By letting go of resistance and limiting beliefs, I make space for the opportunities, love, and abundance that are meant for me.

Every day is filled with gifts, both big and small, and I choose to recognize and appreciate them. I am deserving of the blessings that come my way, and I welcome them with confidence and trust. The more I embrace an open and positive mindset, the more I attract the goodness life has to offer.

Today, I will remain present and receptive to the infinite possibilities around me. Whether it's a kind gesture, an unexpected opportunity, or a moment of peace, I will celebrate every blessing with a grateful heart. I know that the universe is always working in my favor.

By being open to receiving life's blessings, I align myself with abundance and joy. I trust that I am supported, loved, and guided toward my highest good. Infinite blessings surround me, and I welcome them with grace and gratitude.

Morning Prompt

How can you trust the process of abundance today?

Evening Prompt

Reflect on a moment of trust in abundance today.
How did it feel?

Balance

BALANCE

Introduction

Balance is not about perfection—it's about presence. It's about finding rhythm in the way you move through life. Like a garden, you can't water every flower at the exact same time with the exact same amount. Some days require more attention to your rest. Other days, your creativity might need space to bloom. Balance is not a formula—it's a flow, a gentle and intentional return to yourself.

When I was younger, I believed balance meant doing everything equally—dividing my time, energy, and focus into perfect slices of the day. But as I've grown into adulthood, I've learned that balance isn't about having it all together all the time—it's about making time for what truly

matters. It's not about being 50/50 in everything, but about knowing what season you're in and what needs your care the most at that moment. Just like tending to a garden, balance means checking in on your roots: Am I overwatering one part of my life while forgetting to nourish another?

Balance, to me, is making space for what fuels me: my passions, my health, my relationships, my boundaries, and my peace. It's learning when to pour in and when to pull back. It's not just about eating right or getting enough sleep —though those are important—it's about making intentional choices that allow me to grow without burning out. Whether that means saying "no" to a plan so I can rest, or saying "yes" to something new that lights me up, balance is about honoring both structure and softness.

When Life Felt Out of Balance

I didn't always understand what balance really meant. There was a time when I truly believed I was doing everything "right." I had a steady job, friends, and a solid routine. But deep down, something felt off. I was working so hard to maintain a version of life that looked balanced on the outside, but inside, I felt scattered, anxious, and emotionally drained. I thought I was building stability—but what I was really building was burnout.

For a while, I fell into the trap of societal expectations. I let the voices around me steer me—friends, social media, the world telling me what "success" or a "happy life" should look like. I tried following paths that weren't mine, trying to fit into boxes that didn't match my dreams. And even though I smiled through it, I could feel myself losing parts of who I was. I delayed my goals. I ignored my inner voice. I was living someone else's version of balance—not my own.

It wasn't until I took a step back, looked inward, and reconnected with my purpose that I began to rebuild. I realized that balance is not about keeping everything equal. It's about keeping everything aligned. And alignment only comes when you are honest with yourself about what you need, what you love, and what truly fills you up. No job, title, relationship, or schedule is worth sacrificing your peace. No amount of income or approval can replace the feeling of living in your truth.

Creating Boundaries, Finding Balance

One of the most powerful tools I've used to protect my balance is boundaries. We cannot bloom fully when everyone else is pulling at our petals. I've learned to set limits—not because I don't care, but because I do. I care about my energy. My time. My purpose.

In my work life, I try to stay disciplined. If I'm off the clock, I do not check emails. I don't respond to calls unless it's urgent. My rest is not a reward—it's a requirement. I give myself permission to unplug, to pause, to enjoy simple pleasures without guilt. I've also learned to set boundaries in my personal life—when someone wants to hang out but I need time to recharge, I say no kindly and confidently. When people try to pull me off track from my goals or pressure me into saying yes to things that don't align,

Some of the other ways I practice balance include:

- Time blocking my tasks so that my day has structure but not suffocation

- Journaling each night to check in with how I'm feeling and what's on my mind
- Scheduling joy into my week—walks in nature, cozy nights in, or creating content that lights me up
- Checking in with myself every Sunday: What drained me this week? What refueled me? What do I want more of next week?

Balance isn't about doing everything perfectly. It's about being intentional with your yes and powerful with your no.

Let Balance Guide Your Bloom

If your life feels heavy, rushed, or like you're constantly playing catch-up, pause for a moment. Breathe. Reflect. You might not need to push harder—you might just need to recenter. Our culture often glorifies overworking, over-committing, and staying busy as proof of success. But the truth is, burnout is not a badge of honor. Chaos is not a requirement for growth. Sometimes, the most productive thing you can do is slow down.

Balance is not a one-time achievement—it's a daily intention. A conscious choice to check in with yourself and realign your life with what matters. Think of your life as a garden: some days, certain areas will need more water. Other days, you'll need to prune the things that are no longer serving you. Your energy, like sunlight, must be given to what's growing—not to what's draining you. Balance is knowing when to push and when to pause. When to speak and when to listen. When to hold on and when to let go.

Living a balanced life doesn't mean every moment is perfectly divided or always peaceful. It means that you are rooted in your truth—able to recognize when something is off and confident enough to adjust. It means that you're no longer waiting for the world to give you permission to rest, to take up space, or to move at your own pace. You're creating a rhythm that feels sustainable, whole, and real for you. And that's not selfish—that's sacred.

When you allow balance to guide your decisions, your relationships begin to shift. You stop people-pleasing out of guilt and start showing up from a place of honesty. You begin to protect your peace without needing to explain it. You say no to things that once felt like obligations, and yes to things that fill your soul. And most importantly—you stop living your life for appearances, and start living from alignment.

You deserve to create a life that honors both your ambition and your healing. A life that holds space for deep rest and bold action. That allows you to be soft and strong, structured and spontaneous, grounded and still growing. When balance leads the way, you move with more clarity. You show up more fully. You love more deeply. And your presence becomes more powerful—because it's no longer fragmented.

So if you're in a season of imbalance, be gentle with yourself. You're not broken—you're just being invited to bloom differently. You're being reminded to water your roots. To re-center. To return home to yourself. Let balance be your sunlight, your soil, and your steady hand. And trust that as you tend to your inner garden, you are creating a life that doesn't just survive—but flourishes.

Because you were never meant to be in a constant state of survival. You were meant to thrive, to blossom, and to

grow in the direction of your truest, most peaceful self. Let balance guide your bloom—and watch how beautifully your life begins to unfold.

Day 56

"I create balance in my life by honoring my needs and priorities."

Balance is not about perfection—it's about creating harmony between the different aspects of my life. I recognize that my well-being matters, and I choose to honor my needs and priorities without guilt or hesitation. By setting boundaries and listening to myself, I create space for what truly matters.

I understand that balance looks different for everyone, and it may shift as my life changes. That's okay. What's important is that I stay in sync with my physical, emotional,

and mental well-being. When I take care of myself, I am better equipped to show up for my responsibilities and the people I care about.

Today, I will assess my needs and make decisions that support my sense of balance. Whether it's taking time to rest, saying no to overcommitment, or focusing on a goal that aligns with my priorities, I will act with intention. I remind myself that balance is a dynamic process, not a fixed state.

By honoring my needs and priorities, I create a life that feels fulfilling and sustainable. I trust that by nurturing my inner peace, I can achieve my goals while maintaining joy and alignment. Balance is my choice, and I embrace it with grace and care.

Morning Prompt

What is one area of your life that needs balance today?
How will you create it?

_____

_____

_____

_____

_____

_____

_____

_____

_____

_____

_____

_____

_____

_____

_____

_____

_____

_____

_____

_____

_____

_____

Evening Prompt

Reflect on how balanced your day felt. What adjustments could you make tomorrow to improve harmony?

_____

_____

_____

_____

_____

_____

_____

_____

_____

_____

_____

_____

_____

_____

_____

_____

_____

_____

_____

_____

Day 57

"I find harmony by aligning my actions with my values."

Living in alignment with my values brings clarity and peace to my life. When my actions reflect what truly matters to me, I feel grounded, authentic, and fulfilled. I remind myself that harmony isn't about doing everything—it's about doing the right things that resonate with my core beliefs and purpose.

Aligning my actions with my values helps me prioritize what's meaningful and let go of distractions or obligations that don't serve me. It empowers me to make decisions

that honor my integrity and create a sense of balance and flow in my life.

Today, I will reflect on my values and use them as a guide for my choices and actions. Whether in my work, relationships, or personal growth, I will ensure that what I do aligns with who I am and what I stand for. By doing so, I cultivate harmony in my mind, body, and soul.

When my actions align with my values, I move through life with purpose and intention. This alignment creates a sense of fulfillment that radiates outward, enhancing every aspect of my journey. I trust that living authentically will always lead me toward harmony and joy.

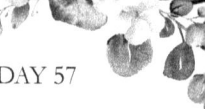

Morning Prompt

What value will guide your actions today?
How can you stay aligned with it?

_____

_____

_____

_____

_____

_____

_____

_____

_____

_____

_____

_____

_____

_____

_____

_____

_____

_____

_____

Evening Prompt

Did your actions today reflect your core values?
How did this affect your sense of harmony?

_____

_____

_____

_____

_____

_____

_____

_____

_____

_____

_____

_____

_____

_____

_____

_____

_____

_____

Day 58

"My mind, body, and spirit work together in perfect balance."

I am a whole and complete being, and I honor the connection between my mind, body, and spirit. When these parts of me are in harmony, I feel centered, strong, and at peace. I recognize that each plays an essential role in my well-being, and I nurture them with care and intention.

My mind provides clarity and focus, my body carries me through each day with strength and resilience, and my spirit connects me to purpose and joy. I commit to giving

each of these aspects the attention they deserve, trusting that balance will naturally follow.

Today, I will make choices that support the alignment of my mind, body, and spirit. Whether it's engaging in self-reflection, nourishing my body with healthy food, moving with intention, or taking moments for stillness and connection, I will act with balance in mind.

By fostering harmony within myself, I create a strong foundation for growth, love, and fulfillment. My mind, body, and spirit work together in perfect balance, supporting me as I navigate life with strength, grace, and authenticity. This balance is my source of power and peace.

Morning Prompt

What can you do today to nurture your mind,
body, and spirit equally?

Evening Prompt

How did you care for your mind, body, and spirit today?
Which area needs more attention?

_____

_____

_____

_____

_____

_____

_____

_____

_____

_____

_____

_____

_____

_____

_____

_____

_____

_____

_____

_____

_____

_____

Day 59

"I protect my energy by maintaining healthy boundaries."

My energy is a precious resource, and I honor it by setting boundaries that align with my well-being. Maintaining healthy boundaries is not selfish—it is an act of self-care and respect. By protecting my energy, I create space for what truly matters in my life.

Boundaries allow me to say yes to what uplifts and nourishes me and no to what drains or overwhelms me. They empower me to prioritize my needs without guilt, knowing that I cannot pour from an empty cup. I

recognize that protecting my energy is essential to living a balanced and fulfilling life.

Today, I will communicate my boundaries with clarity and confidence. I will trust that those who respect and care for me will honor them, and I will release any fear of judgment or rejection. My well-being is my responsibility, and I choose to protect it.

By maintaining healthy boundaries, I cultivate peace, balance, and a deeper connection to myself. I trust that these boundaries not only protect my energy but also allow me to show up more fully and authentically in all areas of my life. My energy is sacred, and I guard it with care and love.

Morning Prompt

What boundary will you set or reinforce today
to protect your energy?

_____

_____

_____

_____

_____

_____

_____

_____

_____

_____

_____

_____

_____

_____

_____

_____

_____

_____

_____

_____

Evening Prompt

*How did maintaining boundaries impact your
sense of balance today?*

_____

_____

_____

_____

_____

_____

_____

_____

_____

_____

_____

_____

_____

_____

_____

_____

_____

_____

_____

_____

_____

_____

Day 60

"I embrace both productivity and rest as essential parts of my day."

I recognize that my well-being thrives on balance. Productivity allows me to pursue my goals, accomplish tasks, and create a sense of fulfillment. Rest gives me the energy, clarity, and peace needed to sustain that productivity. Both are equally valuable and essential to living a harmonious life.

I release any guilt associated with resting, knowing that it is not a sign of weakness but a necessary part of my self-care. By allowing myself time to recharge, I honor my

body, mind, and spirit. Rest enables me to show up more fully for the work and passions that matter to me.

Today, I will approach my day with intention, ensuring that I dedicate time to both focused effort and mindful rest. Whether it's taking a short break, pausing for deep breaths, or setting aside time to unwind, I will create space for rest without hesitation.

By embracing both productivity and rest, I create a sustainable rhythm that supports my growth and well-being. I trust that balance between action and stillness will guide me toward a life of purpose, health, and joy. Rest and productivity are not opposites—they are partners in my success.

Morning Prompt

*What is one productive task and one restful activity
you will prioritize today?*

_____

_____

_____

_____

_____

_____

_____

_____

_____

_____

_____

_____

_____

_____

_____

_____

_____

_____

_____

Evening Prompt

How well did you balance productivity and rest today?
What could you improve?

What's Next?

❁ **The Blossom Podcast: Real stories & reminders of transformation tips & hope for students.**
Be a Guest!

❁ **Workshops & Retreats: Immersive, practical experiences for growth.**
Book Me for In-Person or Virtual workshops for Female Students in Middle, Highschool & College/Trades School (Ages 11 - 19)!

❁ **Assemblies & Youth Groups: Inspiring talks that plant seeds of self-care & self management.**
Invite me to speak as a guest Speaker, Keynote or to provide inspiring insight at your next school assembly, including award ceremonies.

❁ **Blossom Circles with Zara™: Guided journaling & reflection for student communities.**
Sign-Up to start a Blossom Circle for your school, youth group or organization. A perfect wrap-around program.

❁ **The Blossom Letter Newsletter: Weekly inspiration and reminders for growth.**
Sign Up for Resources + Inspirational Content for your student community.

HER Blooming SEASON

Wheel of Becoming